VENISON WISDOM
Cookbook

200 Delicious and Easy-to-Make Recipes

Tracy L. Schmidt

Published by

Krause Publications, a division of F+W Media, Inc.
700 East State Street • Iola, WI 54990-0001
715-445-2214 • 888-457-2873
www.krausebooks.com

To order books or other products call toll-free 1-800-258-0929
or visit us online at www.krausebooks.com

Library of Congress Control Number: 20010925007

ISBN-13: 978-1-4402-1386-1
ISBN-10: 1-4402-1386-0

Designed by Kara Grundman
Edited by Corrina Peterson

Printed in the United States of America

Dedication

❖ ❖ ❖ ❖ ❖

To Dan, Taylor & Emily a.k.a. Team Schmidt

Acknowledgments

❖ ❖ ❖ ❖ ❖

Thanks to the following people who have helped make this project a reality:

- Dan, Taylor and Emily. Thanks for your patience, support and smiles at the end of the hard days. You are all inspirational and great blessings in my life.

- Mom and Dad Schubert. Thanks for all your help during 2009.

- Pa and Grandma Helen. I wish you all the best in your new beginning.

- Tony Schmidt. Thanks for all your help back in the day.

- Robyn, Lisa and the staff of the Iola Village Library, for keeping my children well supplied with books to keep them happy while I work from home.

- To you. Thank you for buying, reading and using this book.

Special thanks go to all the friends, family and inspirational people who contributed recipes to this book.

Contents

Foreword

As a full-time outdoor journalist, I've seen many "how-to" books written about hunting the whitetail. For the most part, these titles are very comprehensive and share all kinds of tips on how to hone one's deer-hunting skill. Unfortunately, few share what to do after the trophy has been harvested. Even fewer address how to turn venison into world-class cuisine. This is sad because venison is not only the healthiest red meat a person can consume but also very tasty if prepared correctly.

This has all changed because you are now holding what I believe is the best venison cookbook ever published. My reasons for feeling this way are many. For starters, *Venison Wisdom* is authored by a gal who knows what she is talking about. Tracy Schmidt is not only a great cook but also an avid whitetail hunter. Furthermore, Tracy happens to be married to one of America's foremost whitetail hunters and magazine editors, Dan Schmidt, Editor of *Deer & Deer Hunting Magazine*.

The Schmidts come from a long line of Wisconsin deer hunters who know how to turn venison into five-star meal offerings. Within this book, you will find not only Tracy's Top 100 venison recipes but also those of family and friends who are great deer hunters. You will also find favorite venison recipes from some of the hunting industry's biggest names — Ted Nugent, Mark Drury, R.G. Bernier, Dr. Phillip Bishop, Les Davenport, Bob Robb and a whole lot more.

When it comes to venison, no stone has been left unturned in this book. In addition to the great recipes, you'll find 100 tips that cover everything from venison nutrition and meat processing to blood-trailing tactics. So, sit down and study *Venison Wisdom* carefully because it is not only a cookbook, it is also a healthy-living manual. Once you dish up one of Tracy's recipes, you'll realize just how precious and delicious venison is.

Enjoy. You are in for a real treat!

Charles J. Alsheimer
Contributing Editor & Television Host
Deer & Deer Hunting Magazine

Key to Meatcuts

Bcn Bacon   **Chp** Chops   **RB** Ring Bologna   **Sge** Sausage

Brt Brat   **Grd** Ground   **Rst** Roast   **Stk** Steak

Introduction

◇◈◇◈◇◈◇◈◇

Why this book? How will it help you be a better cook, hunter and community member? Read on to learn how this book has given me all of these gifts.

This book exists because I took a leap of faith and followed my heart.

I walked away from a 12-year career as an antiques & collectibles editor to stay home with my youngest daughter. I did much soul searching to figure out where my next steps should fall. I concluded that they best fell in a comfortable pair of old shoes: cooking and hunting.

I am a cook and a baker, not a chef. I spent many hours of my youth watching Julia Child, Jeff Smith and Mary Ann Esposito on the local PBS channel. I loved to bake cakes, sweets and breads and make candy. I learned how to "wing it" in the kitchen during my financially meager college years, which is when I moved to Wisconsin from the Boston suburbs and started having a garden. I made and froze a lot of vegetable soup and worked summers at a local farm market, where I learned a great deal about gardening and growing herbs.

Today, I have a 5,000-square-foot garden full of asparagus, berries, beans, carrots, corn, herbs, garlic, onions, potatoes and many other vegetables. I start many of my plants from seed in my greenhouse, and can and freeze food every year.

My love of hunting began with my husband, Dan. His enthusiasm for the sport is contagious, and he has taken me on many adventures in our time together. He taught me how to shoot a bow and arrow and 12-gauge slug gun. He also taught me how to blood trail deer and drag them out of about every place imaginable, including a few thorn-nasty blackberry patches.

Hunting with Dan was hard when I was a beginner. I'd take a vacation day from work to sit down in a ground blind. About two hours after I was settled and jumping out of my skin in anticipation, Dan would show up to get me to trail a deer he shot. I remember a few tense moments along the way, because while I was happy for him, dang it, I wanted a turn to try too! Ten years of marriage later, we have survived and forged a true camaraderie in the field. And, yes, I do get to shoot some deer too.

As a result of Dan's enthusiasm for hunting, he has brought me home a ton of venison that I had to learn how to cook. We survived that learning curve as well, from the tough overcooked leather to learning that there is more to do with venison than stuff it in a taco shell. We then had two daughters who I needed to get enthused about eating venison.

Venison Wisdom is a compilation of all the phases of my life and my evolution into being a better hunter, cook and outdoors community member. The purpose of this cookbook is to provide recipes to cooks looking to prepare flavorful, feel-good dishes out of venison, the world's healthiest red meat.

Venison Wisdom is organized the way I like to cook, which is by not having to spend hours going through a cookbook full of things I don't want to eat. If you hate mushrooms, with my book you can skip that section. If you love tomato flavors, head there.

Dan's *Venison Wisdom* tips cover everything from nutrition to meat processing and venison history to proven blood-trailing tactics. The tips provide great conversational information for dinnertime.

Please remember that all venison roasts are not created equal. There are often no weights on the packages, so I have done my best to be accurate by cooking all of the recipes, but there are some natural variances that will occur, as you are dealing with a product straight from nature.

I would also like to share this old family recipe with you. It comes from Dan's Grandma Schmidt, who handed it down to his mother, Chrisanthia, in the winter of 1954. For health reasons, I suggest leaving out the bacon grease from the sauce when you prepare it. Perhaps give it a try with some venison bacon. It's your call, since all great family recipes evolve with time, as they should.

◇◇◇◇◇◇

Bcn *Grandma Dora Schmidt's Gravy Bread*

6 cups milk, divided
6 tablespoons cornstarch
16 or 18 slices bacon (fry till crisp and crumble)
salt and pepper to taste

Put 5-1/2 cups milk in saucepan. Add cornstarch that has been mixed with 1/2 cup milk and stir until thickens, add bacon that has been crumbled up and the bacon grease. Add salt and pepper and serve over toast.

Happy eating!

For more tips, recipes and chat, visit my Web site: www.venisonwisdom.com

Tracy's Top 100

❖ ◇ ❖ ◇ ❖ ◇

Chapter 1:

Herbed, Seasoned & Spiced

Brt *Oktoberfest Brats*

My German heritage makes me yearn for the tasty blend of onion, beer and brats throughout the summer and fall. I like the flavor of a hearty bock in this meal.

Serves: 6

6 venison brats	1 can beer
1 tablespoon butter	pepper
1/2 cup onion, diced	6 buns

In skillet, add butter, pepper and onion and cook until soft. Add brats and cook until browned. Pour beer into skillet and simmer over low heat, turning brats over until heated through. Place in buns and top with the softened onions.

THE SECRET TO FREEZING MEAT

Using a common method from commercial food processors can make the difference between above-average venison and the best you've ever had. The technique is called "flash freezing," and it can be easily accomplished with most of today's chest-style and upright freezers. Flash freezing is accomplished by placing freshly cut and packaged venison into a freezer set at minus 15 degrees. The key is to set the freezer to its coldest setting several hours before processing your venison. The fast freezing action instantly seals in flavor, retaining those qualities for up to six months in cold storage. High-end freezers can take this one step further with "blast freezing." This is accomplished when meat is frozen at minus 20 degrees. Blast freezing eliminates the problem of having ice crystals form in the meat fibers.

Chp *Fried Venison Chops*

Planning ahead and allowing an overnight marinate allows the buttermilk enzymes to tenderize the meat.

Serves: 6

6 boneless venison chops
1-1/2 cups buttermilk
1-1/2 cups flour
1-1/2 teaspoons salt

1/4 teaspoon pepper
1-1/2 teaspoons garlic powder
vegetable oil for frying

Pound venison chops with a mallet until they are 1/4-inch thick. Place chops in buttermilk to marinate overnight. In a bowl, combine flour, salt, pepper and garlic powder. Remove venison from buttermilk and dredge in dry mixture. Cook the venison in hot oil in fryer to desired doneness.

Grd *4 a.m. Wraps*

These are a great breakfast treat for hunting mornings and busy family weekends. To save even more time, prepare the onions, green peppers and taco meat the night before.

Serves: 4

1/2 pound venison, ground
8 eggs
1/2 cup cheddar cheese
1/4 cup onion, minced
1/4 cup milk

2 tablespoons green pepper, diced
water
taco seasoning packet
1 package tortillas
1 jar salsa

In skillet, brown ground venison, drain fat, and add taco seasoning and water per package instructions. In medium bowl, whisk eggs and milk, then add onions and peppers. Cook in a skillet until eggs begin to set. Add meat filling and cheese and continue to cook, scrambling until done. Serve rolled up in warm tortilla with salsa.

PAPER OR PLASTIC?

When it comes to packaging your food, insist on paper. Food-grade freezer paper is the best choice for packaging most red meats, especially venison. In an effort to save money, some hunters use plastic bags, which are economical and easier to use. Plastic is a poor choice. Plastic bags not only retain moisture — which leads to ice crystals in the meat — non-food-grade bags are often laced with toxins. For example, many black garbage bags are made from petroleum and recycled materials, which can leach into the meat. If you must use plastic bags, be sure to choose those that are approved for food storage.

Grd *Bacon Meatloaf*

This mixture seems a bit soupy prior to baking, but the end result is a moist, firm loaf.

Serves: 8

1-1/2 pounds venison, ground	dash pepper
1 small onion, minced	1/2 teaspoon salt
2 eggs	2 teaspoons chili powder
1 14 oz can diced tomatoes	2 large cloves garlic, minced
1/4 cup sweet green pepper, diced	4 thick slices of bacon
2 slices of bread, cubed	

Preheat oven to 350 degrees.
In large bowl, place all ingredients except bacon. Mix and place in loaf pan. Pat it flat and layer the bacon strips over the top of the loaf. Place loaf on a cookie sheet to catch any drips. Bake for 90 minutes.

Grd *Bacon-Stuffed Burgers*

My kids love the bacon surprise inside these burgers. I find it easiest to divide the mixed meat into fourths and then shape it into mini-loaves. I divide those in half, and the subsequent halves again, creating 16 proportionate patties.

Serves: 8

1 pound venison, ground	1/4 cup shredded cheddar
1 pound pork, ground	1/2 teaspoon pepper
4 bacon strips	1/2 teaspoon garlic powder
1/2 cup sliced mushrooms, optional	2 tablespoons Worcestershire sauce
1/3 cup onion, chopped	8 hamburger buns

In large skillet, cook bacon until crisp. Remove bacon, pat off the grease with paper towels, and crumble the bacon in a bowl. Remove most of the drippings from the skillet, leaving just enough to sauté the onion. Add the mushrooms and crumbled bacon to the sautéed onions and set aside. Combine remaining ingredients except buns in a large bowl and shape into 16 patties. Place the mushroom, onion and bacon mix on top of eight of the patties in the center. Place the other patties on top and pinch edges to seal. Grill until done.

LESS FAT, FEWER CALORIES
Fat comes in three basic forms: saturated, polyunsaturated and monounsaturated. Fat from animal meat is the most dangerous. Cholesterol content is the other key in determining a meat's health status. Surprisingly, a 3.5-ounce serving of normal ground beef has 40 percent more calories, 223 percent more fat, and 125 percent more cholesterol than the same amount of ground venison. Venison is also far healthier than lean ground beef. Lean ground beef still has 31 percent more calories, 189 percent more fat and 118 percent more cholesterol than an equal amount of venison.

Grd *Chili with Bacon*

The smoky flavors in this chili make it my personal favorite. In fact, it is more smoky than spicy. If you like a little more heat, add a can of chopped green chili peppers.

Serves: 6

1 pound venison, ground
4 slices thick bacon, diced
3/4 cup onion, diced
1/4 cup sweet green pepper, diced
2 15 oz cans red kidney beans,
   drained and rinsed

2 14 oz cans diced tomatoes
1 clove garlic, minced
1-1/4 teaspoons salt
1 tablespoon chili powder
pepper

In 6-quart stockpot, add bacon and cook until crisp. Remove pieces and drain on paper towels. Add onion and green pepper to grease in pot and cook until soft but not brown. Add venison and cook until browned. Remove drippings. Add beans, garlic, salt, chili powder, tomatoes, pepper and bacon. Cover pot and simmer for 15 minutes. Uncover and simmer an additional 45 minutes until thickened.

Grd *Citrus Surprise Quarter-Pounders*

I microwave the lime whole for 10-15 seconds on high, then press on it and roll it on the counter to make juicing it easier.

Serves: 4

1 pound venison, ground
1 egg
2 tablespoons olive oil
1 tablespoon rice wine vinegar
1 tablespoon red cooking wine
3 cloves garlic, minced

2 teaspoons sugar
1/4 teaspoon salt
1/4 cup dry bread crumbs, plain
1/2 lime, juiced
4 hamburger buns

In large bowl, combine olive oil, rice wine vinegar, red cooking wine, garlic, sugar, salt, bread crumbs, egg and lime juice. Add the ground venison and shape into four burger patties. Place cooked burgers on buns.

A NATURAL CURE FOR HEADACHES
   Do you suffer from migraines? Eat more venison! According to scientific studies, the levels of riboflavin in venison might actually help reduce the occurrence of migraine attacks by improving the energy metabolism of human cells. According to the studies, riboflavin, which is also known as Vitamin B-2, attaches to protein enzymes to help boost energy. A 4-ounce cut of venison steak, roast and/or loin includes about .68 milligrams of riboflavin, which is 40 percent of an adult's daily recommended allowance.

(Grd) *Emily's Meatloaf Special*

This dish is not hot, but it is spicy. To make it even sharper, use a hot salsa and substitute a can of chopped chili peppers for the sweet green pepper. You can also increase the amount of red pepper flakes and add another teaspoon of chili powder.

Serves: 6

2 pounds venison, ground
1 small onion, minced
2 eggs
1 14 oz can diced tomatoes
1/4 cup sweet green pepper, diced
2 slices of bread, cubed
dash pepper
1/2 teaspoon salt

2 teaspoons chili powder
1/2 teaspoon ground cumin
1/4 teaspoon crushed red
  pepper flakes
2 cloves garlic, minced
1 jar mild salsa
1 cup cheddar cheese, shredded

Preheat oven to 350 degrees.
In large bowl, place all ingredients except ketchup. Mix together, form loaf and place it diagonally in a 9-inch x 9-inch cake pan. Bake for 50 minutes, then spread enough salsa over the top to cover the loaf and bake another 20 minutes, add cheddar cheese to top and return to the oven for an additional 15 minutes or until thoroughly cooked and juices run clear.

(Grd) *Fiesta Burgers*

Cheddar cheese is a great substitute for pepper jack cheese if you prefer a milder flavor.

Serves: 4

1 pound venison, ground
1/4 cup onion, minced
1 package taco seasoning
4 slices pepper jack cheese

4 hamburger buns
1 jar salsa
sour cream

In mixing bowl, blend venison, onion and taco seasoning. Form into patties and cook on grill or in skillet to desired doneness. Top with pepper jack cheese and place on bun. Add salsa on top of cheese and cover with bun top, spread with sour cream.

CUT THE FAT
   Most internal fat on a deer carcass will be found inside the stomach cavity lining the spine and in the pelvic region of the hams. For best venison flavor, remove all traces of internal fat. This can be done immediately upon field-dressing, which assists in fat removal because the fat accumulations are warm and easy to pull free of the carcass. Fat can also be peeled away after the carcass has been cooled. A long-bladed fillet knife greatly assists in this process.

Grd *Scandinavian Meatballs*

The cornstarch in this recipe acts as a thickener and helps hold the meatballs together. The easiest way to turn the meatballs is with a spoon. It is important to not over-manipulate the meatballs, as they will break apart.

Serves: 6

1-1/2 pounds venison, ground
1 egg, slightly beaten
3/4 cup milk
2 tablespoons cornstarch
1 large onion, diced
1/2 teaspoon salt

pepper
1/4 teaspoon ground nutmeg
1/4 teaspoon ground allspice
1/4 teaspoon ground ginger
3 tablespoons butter

In large bowl, whisk the egg, cornstarch, salt, pepper, spices and milk. Add the onions and venison, mix together and form into meatballs, squeezing out any extra milk as you shape them.

In large skillet, melt butter and brown meatballs in batches for 10 minutes or until cooked through. Remove meatballs and drain on paper towels. Remove drippings from skillet and return meatballs to reheat. Add sauce.

Sauce
2 tablespoon butter
4 tablespoons flour

2-1/2 cups beef broth
2/3 cup light cream

In saucepan, melt butter. Add flour and cook until lightly browned. Add broth and light cream all at once, whisking vigorously until thick and bubbly. Salt and pepper to taste.

Grd *Swamp Buck Chili Mac*

This recipe produces a chili that is thick, rather than soupy, and includes macaroni.

Serves: 8

1 pound venison, ground
2 14 oz cans tomatoes, diced
1 6 oz can tomato paste
1 package taco seasoning
2 teaspoons ground cumin
1 15 oz can red kidney beans

1 15 oz can whole kernel corn
1 small can chopped chili peppers
2 tablespoons instant tapioca
1 package macaroni and cheese,
   prepared according to package
   directions

In skillet, brown venison. Drain fat and add the meat to the slow cooker. Add the remaining ingredients except macaroni and cheese and cook for 5 hours. When chili is cooked, add macaroni and cheese.

(Grd) *Tangy Taco Salad*

I make this regularly in the fall as a deer camp snack or football treat. It is visually attractive and fun to eat. Sometimes I just put out a bag of chips and all of the ingredients and let everyone create their own plate.

Serves: 8

1 pound venison, ground
1 clove garlic, minced
1 package taco seasoning
3/4 cup water
1 head of lettuce, washed, dried
   and torn into bite-sized pieces
4 oz Mexican cheese blend,
   shredded

1 can sliced black olives
1 14 oz can diced tomatoes, drained
1 bunch scallions, sliced
1 bag of tortilla chips
sour cream
1 4 oz can chopped green chilies

In skillet, brown venison and garlic. Drain fat. Add taco seasoning and water and cook until thickened. On a large serving platter, layer the ingredients as follows: tortilla chips across entire bottom; venison in the center surrounded by lettuce, diced tomato, scallions, chilies and black olives; top venison with blend cheese and sour cream.

(Grd) *Taylor Lake Casserole*

We serve this dish with sour cream and additional salsa on the side.

Serves: 8

1 pound venison, ground
1 jar of salsa
1 package taco seasoning

3/4 cup water
3 cups crushed tortilla chips
2 cups cheddar cheese, shredded

In skillet, brown venison, drain fat and add taco seasoning with water. Cook until thickened, then add salsa. Spray an 11-inch x 7-inch baking pan with non-stick cooking spray. Layer the ingredients in the pan as follows: 1/2 of the crushed tortilla chips, 1/2 meat mixture and 3/4 cup cheddar cheese. Repeat layering. Top with remaining 1/2 cup of cheddar and bake about 20 minutes until top cheese is nicely browned. Stir before serving.

KEEP YOUR DEER STRESS-FREE

Deer that are pushed hard before being harvested tend to produce less desirable venison. This holds especially true with deer that run long distances after being shot. The reasons behind this phenomenon have to do with sudden surges of adrenalin in the bloodstream. According to research conducted at Utah State University, adrenalin accelerates the deer's heartbeat and constricts visceral blood vessels. This chemical-physiological chain reaction then floods the deer's muscles with blood which, in turn, produces a build-up of lactic and pyruvic acids.

🅁🅑 *Buck Bologna in Beer*

Serve this dish with mashed potatoes on the side and green beans for a great meal with friends.

Serves: 4

1 venison ring bologna	1 can beer
1 tablespoon butter	2 tablespoons cornstarch
1/2 cup onion, diced	pepper
1/4 cup sweet red pepper, diced	

In skillet, add butter and ring bologna and cook until browned. Remove meat to a clean plate, add vegetables and cook until soft but not brown. Add beer, pepper and cornstarch, blend and bring to a boil. Return ring bologna to skillet and cook until heated through.

🅁🅑 *Opening Day Hash*

Oregano is a great companion flavor to the potatoes in this dish. For this dish, I like to remove the casing and outer skin from the ring bologna before I cube it.

Serves: 6

1 venison ring bologna, cooked and cut into small cubes	3/4 teaspoon dried oregano
2 tablespoons vegetable oil	4 large russet potatoes, peeled and cubed
1 large onion, diced	1 15 oz can whole kernel corn, drained
3 cloves garlic, minced	

In large skillet, sauté onion and garlic in oil until soft but not brown. Add potatoes and cook, stirring occasionally for 20 minutes. Add ring bologna and cook until potatoes are soft on the inside and crispy on the outside. Add corn and oregano then heat through.

IT DOESN'T TASTE LIKE CHICKEN

America's fascination with chicken is well documented, but is our favorite white meat really that much healthier than red meat? Not when you compare it to venison. Even if you disregard the fact that most commercially grown chickens are pumped full of antibiotics and growth-enhancers (steroids), this white meat does not outshine venison from free-ranging deer. For example, a 3-ounce cut of lean venison has 135 calories, 26 grams of protein and 3 grams of fat. The same size cut of chicken breast has 120 calories, 24 grams of protein and 1.5 grams of fat. The chicken is leaner, but it also contains more cholesterol and provides virtually no iron (1 mg.). The cut of venison provides nearly 8 mg of iron.

RB *Ring Bologna & Cheese Bake*

I enjoy the leftovers from this meal every bit as much as the first night I serve it. The kids actually manage to eat their broccoli with a smile in a plateful of this dish.

Serves: 6

1 venison ring bologna cooked
   and cut into bite-size pieces
1 pound broccoli
2 cups milk

4 tablespoons butter
3 tablespoons flour
1-1/2 cups cheddar cheese,
   shredded

Preheat oven to 375 degrees.
Grease a 2-quart casserole. Wash and trim broccoli and cook in boiling water 5 minutes. Drain and pat as much water out as possible with paper towels. Then chop into smaller bite-size pieces. Heat the milk. Melt the butter in a 2-quart saucepan, remove from heat, add flour and stir. Pour in the hot milk and return to heat, cooking until mixture thickens and boils. Add 1 cup cheddar cheese and stir until melted. Spread half of broccoli in casserole. Add half of the cooked ring bologna. Cover with half of the cheese sauce. Repeat the layering and top with the remaining cheddar cheese. Bake for 30 minutes.

Rst *Biscuit Pie*

If you like a quick pot pie without the hassle of a pastry crust, this is the recipe for you.

Serves: 6

3 cups venison, cubed and cooked
1 large onion, sliced
2 tablespoons butter
1/4 cup red cooking wine
1 10-1/2 oz can beef broth

1/4 cup flour
1/2 teaspoon garlic powder
1 teaspoon oregano
1 10 oz package mixed frozen
   vegetables

Preheat oven to 425 degrees.
In large skillet, sauté onion in 2 tablespoons butter until soft but not brown. In large measuring cup, whisk red cooking wine, broth, 1/4 cup flour, garlic powder and oregano and add to skillet. Cook until thickened, then add vegetables and venison. Heat through and pour into 3-quart casserole. Follow directions for topping, then bake for 35-40 minutes, until brown.

Topping

3/4 cup old-fashioned oats,
   uncooked
3/4 cup flour
1/2 teaspoon oregano

2 teaspoons baking powder
6 tablespoons butter
1/2 cup milk
1 egg

In medium bowl, mix oats, flour, oregano and baking powder. Cut in 6 tablespoons butter until it reaches a texture similar to large cornmeal. Add in egg and milk, stir quickly. Drop in large spoonfuls onto top of casserole.

ⓇⓈⓉ *Dan's Basic Roast*

A quick-prep oven-cooked roast made with ease...who wouldn't like that on a cold snowy day or as part of a game-day meal?

Serves: 8

4 pounds of venison roast
2 tablespoons vegetable oil
1 package onion soup mix

1-1/4 cups water
4 tablespoons flour

Brown roast in oil in roasting pan on stove burner. Add soup mix and 1 cup water and cover. Cook over low heat for about 2 to 2-1/2 hours or to desired doneness. Mix 1/4 cup flour and 1/4 cup water and add paste to drippings left in pan after roast is removed. Whisk over low heat until gravy reaches desired thickness.

ⓇⓈⓉ *Marengo River Roast*

This roast will melt in your mouth. I usually start checking for doneness after 90 minutes. My personal target temperature is 172 degrees Fahrenheit, but continue cooking until your desired doneness is reached.

Serves: 6

3-4 pounds of venison roast
1/4 cup dark brown sugar, packed
1 teaspoon dried thyme
1 teaspoon dried garlic powder
1 teaspoon dried rosemary
pepper

1 teaspoon onion powder
salt
1 jar beef gravy (or mix two cups
   beef broth and 1/4 cup flour and
   bring to a boil while whisking)

Preheat oven to 500 degrees.
Combine all ingredients except flour and gravy and rub on roast. Place roast on rack in roasting pan and place uncovered in oven. Immediately lower temperature to 325 degrees. Bake for 2 hours or until cooked. Remove roast from oven and allow to cool. Serve with gravy if desired.

WHY SOME VENISON IS DARKER THAN OTHERS
Have you ever noticed a distinct difference in the color of your fresh venison? Whitetail hunters have reported this phenomenon for years and have been left wondering why venison from deer shot from the same area varies from bright red to dark almost purple. Researchers set out to determine the reasons, and they concluded that it can be directly linked to stress on the animal immediately before it was killed. One of the researchers, Joyce Hosch, reported that venison is often dark red when it comes from deer that are pushed hard and/or left to run long distances before dying. She concluded that the meat enters the rigor mortis stage faster in these cases, hence the color difference. She also noted that cuts of venison from stressed animals tend to be less tender than those from deer that are killed cleanly.

(Sge) *Bucksnort Biscuits & Gravy*

This old-fashioned morning favorite never goes out of style. It is also an economical breakfast, especially if you like to make your own biscuits from scratch.

Serves: 6

1 pound venison sausage	1/8 teaspoon salt
2 tablespoons butter	3-1/2 cups milk
6 tablespoons flour	1 can of refrigerated biscuits,
pepper	prepared

In large saucepan, brown venison, then remove and drain fat from pan. In pan, add butter and flour and cook until browned. Add milk, salt and pepper all at the same time. Serve over prepared biscuits.

(Sge) *Sausage Stuffed Peppers*

These stuffed peppers are a great way to create a visually appealing plate as well as put a great taste in your mouth. They take a little bit of prep work, but are worth the effort.

Serves: 4

3 venison sausages, cooked and sliced thin	1/4 cup onion, chopped
	2 cloves garlic, minced
4 large sweet green peppers, seeds removed	1-1/4 cups packed, cooked rice
	2/3 cup tomato, diced
3 tablespoons butter	salt
2 tablespoons chopped sweet green pepper	pepper
	3/4 cup water

Preheat oven to 350 degrees.
Blanch peppers in boiling water 5 minutes, remove and drain.
In skillet, melt 2 tablespoons butter and add green pepper, onion and garlic and cook until soft but not brown. Add sausages, rice, tomato, remaining tablespoon of butter, pepper and salt and cook until heated.
Fill peppers with stuffing and place in shallow baking pan. Add water and cover with foil. Bake for 25 minutes then uncover and bake for 15 minutes.

REDUCE EXPOSURE
Venison's lean nature makes it susceptible to dehydration if it is not prepared properly. Any exposure to air causes the meat to dry quickly, which is why most professional processors prefer to butcher their own deer quickly upon harvesting and freeze cuts once the body heat has left the meat tissues. With this in mind, it is recommended that hunters do not split open the pelvic cavity when field-dressing their deer. Splitting open the pelvis not only allows air to taint the uppermost portions of the hams; it invites bacteria growth on what are otherwise choice cuts of meat.

(Stk) *Namakagon Kabobs*

I love the smoky flavor of this dish, and the kabobs go great with a cold beverage after work. The bacon should be crisp when cooked, so make sure to leave some air around the bacon-wrapped meat so it crisps better.

Serves: 4

1 pound venison steak, cubed	8 cherry tomatoes
1 bottle mesquite marinade	1 large onion, wedged
8 bacon strips, halved	skewers, metal or soaked wood
1 large zucchini, chunked	

Place cubed venison in a quart-size plastic bag. Add marinade, reserving 1/2 cup for basting, and let sit overnight. Remove, drain and wrap cubes with bacon. Place meat alternately with vegetables on metal or soaked wooden sewers. Grill 10-15 minutes, basting with reserved sauce.

(Stk) *Marinated Steaks*

This has been one of Dan's favorite marinades for years. The meat is always tender and has a great flavor.

Serves: 2-4

2 venison steaks	1/2 teaspoon salt
1/4 cup red wine vinegar	1 teaspoon dry mustard
1/4 cup ketchup	pepper
2 tablespoons Worcestershire sauce	3 cloves garlic, crushed

Place all ingredients in gallon-size plastic bag except meat. Blend, then reserve 1/2 cup of sauce to use for basting. Add meat to bag and marinate overnight, turning the bag several times during the process. Remove meat from bag, discard marinade, and grill steaks to desired doneness, basting frequently with reserved marinade.

THE VENISON CAPITAL OF THE WORLD

North America might be the whitetail capital of the world, but it is not the venison capital. That title belongs to New Zealand. When whitetails and whitetail hunting were hitting new peaks in the United States in the 1970s, New Zealand red deer farmers were building an industry that is now unrivaled in the world. Today, New Zealand exports approximately 27,000 tons of venison annually. About 85 percent of that total is sent to Europe during the two months preceding Christmas each year. The economic impact is estimated at $260 million a year. Although that is a lot of backstrap, it pales in comparison to New Zealand's beef industry, which generates $2.2 billion annually.

(Stk) *Pepper Steak*

Be sure to slice the meat very thinly using a sharp knife. We often serve this over quick-cook rice, but it would also be great in a sandwich.

Serves: 6

2 pounds venison steak, sliced thin
2 large sweet green peppers, sliced
   into 1/4-inch rings
2 onions, quartered
1 14-1/2 oz can beef broth

2 tablespoons soy sauce
2 teaspoon Worcestershire sauce
2 cloves garlic, minced
3/4 teaspoon ground ginger

Preheat oven to 325 degrees.
Layer ingredients in roasting pan as follows: peppers, meat and onions. Mix other ingredients in a small bowl, then pour sauce into pan. Cook until done, about 2-3 hours.

(Stk) *Pioneer Potluck*

If a stew married a chili and produced a child, this would be it. There is no tomato in this recipe, but the beans and corn are taken from chili and the gravy is like that of a stew.

Serves: 6

2 pounds venison, cubed
1/2 cup flour
pepper and salt
1 teaspoon garlic powder
1/4 cup vegetable oil
1 medium onion, chopped
1 green pepper, chopped

1-1/2 tablespoons chili powder
1 teaspoon dried oregano
1 16 oz can red kidney beans,
   drained and rinsed
1 15 oz can whole kernel corn,
   drained
2 cups water

Combine flour, garlic powder, pepper and salt in a quart-size plastic bag and add venison cubes. Shake to coat evenly. Heat oil in Dutch oven and brown meat. Add green peppers and onions and cook until tender. Stir in seasonings and 2 cups water. Bring to boil, then reduce heat, cover and simmer, stirring often, for about 45 minutes or until tender. Add beans and corn and cook an additional 10 minutes.

GUT SHOT, NOW WHAT?
   When dealing with a deer that has been shot through the paunch, intestines or liver, field-dress the animal promptly, using extra care to wipe off excess blood and stomach matter. When you return to camp, prop the deer's chest up and thoroughly rinse the cavity with a garden hose. If a hose isn't available, use buckets of clean drinking water. Rinse the cavity until it clean of all blood and debris. Next, use paper toweling to remove all moisture from the inside of the cavity. Finally, hang the deer, head up, to assist in further drainage.

Stk *Salsa Wrap*

Our family enjoys this quick-cook meal that is fun for the kids to assemble themselves before eating.

Serves: 4

1 pound venison steak, sliced into
  3/4-inch strips
1/4 cup red wine vinegar
1/4 cup ketchup
3 cloves garlic, crushed

1/4 teaspoon salt
1 cup cheddar cheese, shredded
1 jar salsa
lettuce, shredded
1 package tortillas

Slice steak strips and set aside. In large food storage bag, combine red wine vinegar, ketchup, salt and garlic. Add meat and marinate overnight or at least 45 minutes. Remove meat and discard marinade. Place meat in skillet over medium heat until desired doneness is reached.
Remove meat from skillet and place in tortilla. Add lettuce, shredded cheddar and salsa.

Stk *Smokey Valley Chili*

Dan's favorite chili by far, this is a hearty, robust chili that warms your stomach without making you cry. The tapioca acts as a thickener.

Serves: 5

1-1/2 pounds venison, cubed
1 tablespoon vegetable oil
2 garlic cloves, minced
3 jalapenos, diced
1 cup onion, chopped
2 tablespoons chili powder

2 teaspoons ground cumin
2 teaspoons tapioca
1 28 oz can diced tomatoes with
  roast garlic and onion
1 16 oz can kidney beans, rinsed
  and drained

In stockpot, brown stew meat in oil. Add remaining ingredients, cover and simmer for 3 hours, making sure to stir and add liquid as needed.

TO AGE OR NOT TO AGE?
There is much debate among white-tailed deer hunters over the time-honored tradition of "aging" venison. After years of study and debate, most animal meat scientists agree that venison quality can, in fact, be improved with aging. However, the scientists also agree that a vast majority of hunters lack the proper skills and equipment to age meat safely and effectively. Another point of agreement is that any cuts other than roasts, steaks and chops will not benefit from aging, and that any deer less than 3 years old will not benefit from aging. According to Dr. Robert Wegner, to age properly, venison must be kept in a walk-in style cooler that is kept at a temperature of 34 to 37 degrees with a relative humidity of 88 percent for seven to nine days. The field-dressed carcass should be kept whole. Skinning the carcass will lead to dehydration of the muscle tissues.

Stk *Southwestern Pita*

This sandwich is full of flavor and texture. The cinnamon helps bring out the sweet flavor in the corn, while the cumin adds depth to the whole combination.

Serves: 4

1 pound venison steak, sliced into
  3/4-inch strips
1/4 cup olive oil
1/4 cup rice wine vinegar
1/8 cup red wine
3 cloves garlic, crushed
1 lime, juiced
1 tablespoon sugar
1/4 teaspoon salt
1 can black beans, drained

1 can whole kernel corn, drained
1 can tomatoes, diced
2 scallions, sliced
1/4 cup sweet green pepper,
  chopped
1/4 teaspoon cinnamon
3/4 teaspoon ground cumin
4 pita pockets
lettuce, shredded
sour cream

Slice steak strips and set aside. In large food storage bag, combine olive oil, rice wine vinegar, red wine, garlic, sugar, salt and the lime juice. Add meat and marinate overnight or at least 45 minutes. Remove meat and discard marinade. Place meat in skillet and cook over medium heat to desired doneness. In medium bowl, mix beans, corn, tomatoes, scallions, green peppers, cinnamon and cumin. Spread sour cream on inside of pitas, then fill pita pockets with lettuce, bean mixture and meat.

Top 10 Marinade Musts

1. Red wine vinegar
2. Pineapple juice
3. Lime juice — a little goes a long
   way
4. Apple cider
5. Coffee
6. Ketchup
7. Orange juice
8. Cider vinegar
9. Stout
10. Dijon Mustard

ASSESSING A DAY-OLD CARCASS

If you hunt deer long enough, you will invariably run across a situation where you must leave your deer go overnight before resuming the blood trail. Warm and/or humid weather conditions will dictate the outcome of your venison. As with all deer, avoid cutting the paunch and intestines during field dressing. If the heart, liver or lungs of a day-old shot deer smell the least bit rank or ooze a greenish discharge, do not consume the animal. These are signs of a severe bacterial infection from rotting flesh. If the carcass does not exhibit these telltale signs, dress the animal promptly and cool the carcass to at least 38 degrees F as quickly as possible.

Stk *Steak & Onion Pie*

You can make this filling a day ahead, warm it in the microwave, then put it in the pie pan, cover it with the crust and bake it for dinner when you get home from work for a quick-fix feast.

Serves: 6

1-1/2 pounds venison steak, cubed
2 cloves garlic, minced
1 large onion, sliced
3 tablespoons vegetable oil
1/3 cup flour
1 teaspoon salt
pepper

1/2 teaspoon ground ginger
2 cups hot water
1-1/2 cups potatoes, cubed
1 cup baby carrots, chopped
1 cup frozen peas
refrigerated pie dough

Place flour, salt, pepper and ginger into a quart-size plastic bag. Add cubed meat to the bag and shake it until coated with flour. In stockpot, soften onion in oil. Remove onion and set aside. Add meat to hot oil and brown it. Add water, garlic and the cooked onion, then simmer for one hour.
Preheat oven to 450 degrees.
Add vegetables to stockpot and cook for 30 minutes more. Place meat mixture in a 9-inch x 9-inch baking pan and cover the top with pie dough pressed tight to the edges. Make a few slits to let steam escape.
Bake for 25-30 minutes or until pastry is nicely browned.

Top 12 Items for your Pantry
(or to bring for deer camp when leaving in a hurry)

1. Potatoes
2. Canned mushrooms
3. Rosemary
4. Canned beef broth or bullion
5. Cream of mushroom soup
6. Garlic powder
7. Onions
8. Red wine vinegar
9. Onion soup mix
10. Canned diced tomatoes
11. Canned whole kernel corn
12. Ketchup

BEHOLD THE POWER OF ICE
Cubed ice can save a deer carcass from certain spoilage in warm weather. If butchering or access to a walk-in cooler are not options, lay your field-dressed deer on its back in a shaded area. The back of a vehicle is ok as long as the vehicle is left open for proper air circulation. Pack the chest cavity and inner thighs with bags of cubed ice. Frozen milk jugs filled with water will also suffice. Keep the deer covered with a light plastic tarp to keep away flies and other pests. Use this only as a last-ditch effort until you can get your deer to a processor or refrigeration.

Chapter 2:

Mushroom-Enhanced

(Chp) *Chop Roll-ups*

I like to serve these roll-ups with a side dish of sautéed garden tomatoes, zucchini and onions during the summer. I prefer to use chunky Portabellas because they provide great flavor and texture.

Serves: 6

6 venison chops, separated into
  halves
1-1/2 cups prepared stuffing mix
2 tablespoons extra virgin olive oil
1/2 cup water

1 10-3/4 oz can condensed
  cream of mushroom soup
1 4 oz can chunky Portabella
  mushrooms, drained
toothpicks

Take the 12 chop medallions and pound out with meat hammer until large enough to stuff. Place 1-2 tablespoons prepared stuffing near center, roll up chops and fasten them with toothpicks. Heat oil in skillet and brown roll ups. Add water, mushrooms and soup to skillet. Cover and simmer over low heat 1-1/4 hours or until tender, stirring as needed.

(Grd) *Button-Bustin' Burgers*

Bring extra napkins to the table when you serve these burgers. They taste great and are a lot of fun to eat, but, like eating ribs, they might not be the best choice for a first date.

Serves: 6

1-1/2 pounds venison, ground
2/3 cup milk
1 4 oz can chunky Portabella
  mushrooms, drained

2 10-3/4 oz cans cream of
  mushroom soup
1/2 can water

Preheat oven to 350 degrees
Mix venison with milk and shape into 6 patties. Seal the edges, and place in 3-quart casserole. Mix soup, mushrooms and water and pour over the patties. Bake for 50 minutes or until desired doneness is reached.

WHERE DID VENISON GET ITS NAME?
The word venison is a derivative of the Latin phrase venari ("to hunt"). The term technically refers to the meat of any large-antlered animal, but it is generally reserved for members of the deer family, including whitetails, elk, caribou, red stags and mule deer. In Europe, avid hunters are called venatics.

(Grd) *Keep-It-Simple Casserole*

Thyme is a great herb to use with both venison and mushrooms. It really gives a boost to the flavor of this dish.

Serves: 6

1 pound venison, ground
1 large yellow onion, chopped
1/2 cup sweet green pepper,
   chopped
1 10-3/4 oz can condensed
   cream of mushroom soup
1 cup uncooked quick rice

1 4 oz can chunky Portabella
   mushrooms, drained
1/3 cup soy sauce
2 cups hot water
1/2 teaspoon salt
1/2 teaspoon garlic powder
1-1/2 teaspoons dried thyme

Preheat oven to 350 degrees.
Brown venison, sauté onion and green pepper until soft but not brown, and set aside. Mix remaining ingredients and add to casserole. Then add venison, onions, peppers and mix. Cover casserole and bake for 60 minutes.

(Grd) *Monday Night Subs*

Even though the mix appears dry, there is so much fat in the pork, they are not dry when cooked. I often make the meatballs ahead and freeze them, then all I have to do is heat them in the microwave and prepare the sauce.

Makes: 44 1-inch meatballs

1-1/2 pounds venison, ground
3/4 pound pork, ground
2 tablespoons brown sugar
1 cup sweet onion, diced
1/2 teaspoon salt

1-1/2 cups dry bread crumbs
dash pepper
2 eggs
sub rolls

Preheat oven to 350 degrees.
Mix all ingredients except sub rolls. Form into meatballs and bake for 25-30 minutes until cooked through. Prepare mushroom sauce. Place meatballs into sub rolls and spoon mushroom sauce over the top.

Mushroom Sauce

1/4 cup onion, minced
2 tablespoons olive oil
3 tablespoons flour

1/4 teaspoon dried thyme
1 14 oz can chicken broth
1 4 oz can chunky Portabella
   mushrooms, drained

In skillet, sauté onion in oil until soft not brown. Add flour to make a paste, then add broth and whisk until thicken and bubbly. Add mushrooms and thyme and cook until heated through.

(Grd) *Mushroom Casserole*

Mushroom casserole is a quick-prep dish that fills up your family. Simple yet flavorful, this is also a great dish for parties.

Serves: 6

1 pound venison, ground
2 4 oz cans chunky Portabella
   mushrooms, drained
3 tablespoons butter

2/3 cup onion, minced
1 cup long grain brown rice
1-1/2 cans (approx 16 oz) beef broth

Preheat oven to 350 degrees.
Sauté onions and mushrooms in butter in skillet until onions soften, then place aside. Brown venison burger, then add with mushrooms and onions to casserole. Stir in rice and broth and cook covered for 40-50 minutes until casserole is no longer soupy. Cool for 5 minutes and serve.

(Grd) *Mushroom Veni Loaf*

This is a great straight-forward meatloaf that is large enough to serve to a group of hungry hunters.

Serves: 8

2 pounds venison, ground
1 cup dried bread crumbs
1/4 cup milk
2 eggs, beaten
1 medium onion, diced
2 cloves garlic, minced

1 small can chopped mushrooms,
   drained
pepper
3/4 cup pepper jack cheese,
   shredded

Preheat oven to 350 degrees.
Add all ingredients to large bowl and mix until blended. Mold into loaf and place in roasting pan. Bake for 45 minutes. Remove and cover with sauce, then sprinkle with cheese. Place sauced loaf back into oven for an additional 15 minutes.

Sauce

1 28 oz can crushed tomatoes
   with basil
1 6 oz can tomato paste
1/2 teaspoon salt

pepper
2 teaspoons brown sugar
1 cup water
2 teaspoons dried oregano

In saucepan, mix all ingredients and stir as needed until heated through. Place over meatloaf as directed above.

THE BIOLOGY OF DEER BLOOD
The average white-tailed deer (weighing about 150 pounds on the hoof) carries about 8 pints of blood in its circulatory system. A deer must lose at least 35 percent of its blood volume (just under three pints) for a quick, humane death.

Grd *Swedish Meatballs*

A tribute to local heritage, we had to include this staple dish.

Makes: 40 1-inch meatballs

1 pound venison, ground
1/2 pound pork, ground
2 tablespoons brown sugar
1 large onion, minced
1/2 teaspoon salt
1-1/2 cups dry bread crumbs
dash pepper
2 eggs
1/4 teaspoon cloves

3/4 teaspoon nutmeg
1/4 teaspoon allspice
1/2 teaspoon dried rosemary,
   crushed
1 10-3/4 oz can condensed
   cream of mushroom soup
1/2 soup can water
egg noodles, prepared

Preheat oven to 350 degrees.
Mix spices, sugar, bread crumbs, eggs, onion, salt, pepper and meats. Form into meatballs and brown batches in skillet. Set aside. In small bowl, mix water and soup and place in casserole. Add meatballs, stirring to coat with sauce. Cover casserole and bake 45 minutes. Serve over egg noodles.

Grd *Venison, Mushroom & Broccoli Bake*

A great bake, this dish combines broccoli, mushrooms and venison in a chunky, feel-good meal.

Serves: 6

1/2 venison ring bologna, sliced
1 cup uncooked converted rice
1 pound broccoli, cooked and
   chopped (buy the pre-cut frozen
   to save time)

1 4 oz can chunky Portabella
   mushrooms, drained
1/2 cup mild cheddar cheese,
   shredded
4 tablespoons butter

Prepare rice according to package directions in large saucepan. Add broccoli, ring bologna, butter, mushrooms and cheddar cheese. Heat until cheese is melted and serve.

HANG THEM HIGH
When hanging deer on a buck pole, be sure to hoist the animals well off the ground. A good rule of thumb is to hang the deer so its hoofs are least 4 feet above the ground. This will prevent stray cats, dogs and rodents from contaminating your precious venison. It is also wise to lightly wrap the open chest/stomach cavity with a thin layer of cheesecloth or fine-mesh netting. This will prevent tallow-hungry gray jays, hairy woodpeckers, chickadees and other small birds from defecating inside the carcass.

Rst *Creamed Venison*

This is a great way to use leftover venison roast. The corn and diced meat provide great texture. It tastes great reheated for lunches.

Serves: 4

1-1/2 cups venison, diced and
  cooked
1/4 cup onion, chopped
1 tablespoon olive oil
1 10-3/4 oz can condensed
  cream of mushroom soup

1/2 cup water
1 15 oz can whole kernel corn,
  drained
1/4 teaspoon garlic powder
pepper
3 cups egg noodles, prepared

In skillet, sauté onion in oil until soft but not brown. Add corn, soup, water, venison, garlic powder and pepper. Heat through and serve over prepared noodles.

Rst *Farmhouse Potpie*

This traditional, hearty potpie incorporates modern-day conveniences that enable it to fit right into today's hectic lifestyle.

Serves: 6

3 cups venison, cubed and cooked
1 large onion, quartered
1 can sliced mushrooms, drained
1 cup potato, cooked and diced
1/2 cup baby carrots, cooked
2 tablespoons butter

1/4 cup red cooking wine
1 10-1/2 oz can beef broth
1/4 cup flour
1 teaspoon oregano
prepared pie dough

Preheat oven to 450 degrees.
Sauté onion in 2 tablespoons butter until soft but not brown. Add red cooking wine, broth, 1/4 cup flour and oregano. Cook until thickened then add vegetables, mushrooms and venison. Heat through and pour into prepared pie dough in pie plate, place top crust over pie, add three vent holes and bake for 25-30 minutes or until pastry is browned.

DON'T SKIMP ON THE SALT
  When making homemade venison jerky, do not use less salt than recommended. According to meat scientists at the University of Georgia, salt is a necessary ingredient in cured meats like jerky, because it binds the moisture in the meat and, therefore, any bacteria present on the meat are more quickly killed during the drying process.

Rst *Mushroom & Tater Chow*

You can save yourself some money in most cases by making your own gravy instead of buying the pre-made version at the grocery store. Add 3 tablespoons vegetable oil and 1/3 cup flour to a saucepan and cook to make a roux, whisk in 32 ounces of beef broth and continue cooking until thick and bubbly.

Serves: 8

4 cups venison, cubed and cooked
1 red onion, sliced
1 4 oz can chunky Portabella
   mushrooms, drained
2 cloves garlic, minced
1/2 teaspoon oregano, divided
2 tablespoons vegetable oil

4 cups prepared beef gravy
1 teaspoon instant beef bouillon
   granules
pepper
3 cups prepared instant mashed
   potatoes

Preheat oven to 350 degrees.
Add oil to large skillet. Sauté garlic, onion, mushrooms and 1/4 teaspoon oregano until soft but not brown. Add venison, gravy, bouillon and dash of pepper. When heated through, pour into 3-quart casserole. Mix potatoes and 1/4 teaspoon oregano and place spoonfuls over the top of the meat mixture. Bake uncovered for 45 minutes.

Rst *Noodles & Venison*

It's simple to make, easy to bake and looks great on your plate. To save time, cube your venison the night before you plan to prepare this dish.

Serves: 4

1-1/2 pounds venison, cubed
2 cloves garlic, minced
2 tablespoons olive oil
1 10-3/4 oz can condensed
   cream of mushroom soup

1/2 soup can water
1/4 teaspoon dried rosemary,
   crushed
1/4 teaspoon paprika
egg noodles, prepared

Preheat oven to 350 degrees.
In skillet, brown venison and garlic in butter. In 3-quart casserole, mix water, soup, rosemary and paprika. Add browned meat and bake for 60 minutes until tender. Serve over egg noodles.

BIGGER IS BETTER

Freezing venison in large chunks or sections (instead of individual steaks and chops) helps retain moisture when it is eventually cooked. Larger sections are also easier to process if they are partially frozen, because it is easier to slice into uniform steaks, chops and roasts.

Pocket-Warmer Pasties

I first learned about these meat-filled pastries pronounced "pass-teez" while driving through Michigan's Upper Peninsula. Many towns boast small diners and restaurants selling these hearty local favorites. This classic pie goes great with a cold Wisconsin beer. Remember to use a moister pastry dough, and cut all of your ingredients small so they will fit nicely in your pie and cook through.

Serves: 5

3/4 pound venison, cubed
2 medium russet potatoes, peeled
   and cubed
1 4 oz can chunky Portabella
   mushrooms, drained
1 large carrot, sliced thinly
1/4 cup onion, chopped
1/2 teaspoon salt

1/2 teaspoon dried rosemary leaves,
   crushed
1/2 teaspoon garlic powder
pepper
1 tablespoon butter
2 eggs
1/4 cup milk

Preheat oven to 425 degrees.
In small bowl, mix eggs and milk together. Set aside.
In large bowl, mix venison, potatoes, mushrooms, carrots, onion, salt, rosemary, garlic powder and pepper. Prepare pastry and fill centers with meat and vegetable mixture. Dot each pastry filling with butter. Fold over dough to make a crescent shape and crimp shut with a fork. Make a small slit in each pastie top. Place on large greased cookie sheet with sides, brush with egg wash and bake for 30-35 minutes or until golden.

Pastry

2 cups flour
1/2 teaspoon salt

3/4 cup shortening
1/2 cup ice water, more or less as
   needed

In a medium bowl, whisk flour with salt. Cut in the shortening until coarse. Stir in water with a fork until it can be pressed into a ball. Divide into two pieces, place on plastic wrap, flatten with your hand and wrap. Place in refrigerator for about 30 minutes. Roll out on lightly floured board into 8-inch circles, with the plastic wrap between the rolling pin and the dough so it does not stick. Makes about five circles.

ULTIMATE MEAT YIELD
  A deer that is killed cleanly — with no waste from bullet or broadhead damage — will yield venison totaling about 67 percent of its field dressed weight. Most carcasses, however, do suffer from some loss due to tissue damage. Therefore, a realistic venison yield can be calculated by multiplying the ideal boneless weight by .70. So, if a hunter shoots a 165-pound buck (dressed), it will produce an ideal venison yield of 83 pounds and a realistic yield of 58 pounds.

Stk *Steak Sandwiches*

These taste great on a fresh roll from the local bakery and accompanied by fries or a nice crisp side salad. I like to use diced tomatoes for texture, but you could substitute tomato sauce if needed.

Serves: 4

1 pound venison steak, sliced into thin strips
2 tablespoons vegetable oil
1 4 oz can chunky Portabella mushrooms, drained
1/2 cup beef broth

1 cup sweet green pepper, chopped
1 14 oz can diced tomatoes
1 teaspoon dried thyme
1 medium onion, sliced
sandwich rolls

In skillet, brown venison steak slices in oil. Drain fat, then add remaining ingredients, cover and simmer for 20 minutes or until meat is tender. Place in rolls.

Stk *Super Fast Stir-Fry with Mushrooms*

We love to eat stir-fry after work. The texture and flavor of the vegetables are great, especially when they are in season.

Serves: 4

1 pound venison steak sliced into 1/4-inch pieces
1 large sweet red pepper, sliced
1 medium sweet onion, diced
1 small zucchini, sliced

1 8 oz package fresh baby Portabella mushrooms, sliced
1/4 cup teriyaki sauce
2 tablespoons olive oil
prepared rice

Heat oil in skillet. Add venison steak slices and cook for 2 minutes. Add remaining vegetables and mushrooms and cook another couple of minutes until vegetables are crisp-tender. Add teriyaki sauce. Serve over rice.

FORMULA FOR CARCASS WEIGHT

Hunters who process their venison at home can keep track of their venison yields more accurately by documenting the carcass weights and venison yields from each deer they kill. These numbers will help hunters determine how much meat is lost from a carcass due to spoilage and/or damage. The carcass weight refers to how heavy the deer is after its head and hide are removed. To obtain this number, you will need the field-dressed weight. Next, divide the field-dressed weight by 1.331. For example, a 165-pound field-dressed buck (with no waste) will have a carcass weight of 124 pounds.

Chapter 3:

Soups & Stews

Grd *Meatball Minestrone Soup*

A quick and hearty soup that tastes great after sitting out on your stand all day. Make it ahead of time, and you can simply heat it up and serve it with some garlic bread as your friends return to deer camp. Venison meatballs tend to fall apart, so I recommend baking them. If you are willing to take your chances, brown them right in the stockpot in 3 tablespoons vegetable oil.

Serves: 6

1 pound venison, ground
1 egg, beaten
1/2 teaspoon onion powder
1/4 teaspoon garlic powder
1/4 cup dry bread crumbs
1 15 oz can tomato sauce
2-3/4 cups water

1 16 oz can red kidney beans, rinsed
  and drained
1/2 teaspoon dried oregano
1/2 teaspoon dried thyme
2 tablespoons dried parsley
1/2 cup mini lasagna macaroni

Preheat oven 350 degrees.
In mixing bowl, add venison, egg, onion powder, garlic powder and bread crumbs. Combine and form into 1-inch meatballs. Bake for 25 minutes, then put meatballs in stockpot. Add tomato sauce, water, kidney beans and seasonings, then simmer covered for 25 minutes. Add macaroni and cook uncovered for an additional 10-12 minutes until pasta is tender.

BE CAREFUL WITH JERKY
From ground-venison shooters to dried strips of "instant lunch," deer jerky is a staple among hunters everywhere. We all love it, but are you being 100 percent safe with your jerky-making practices? According to the United States Department of Agriculture, many hunters are not, and they are putting their health at risk. The USDA warns its hunters not to eat any venison jerky that has not been heated to an internal temperature of 165 degrees BEFORE the drying process. Doing so helps prevent illnesses due to Salmonella and E. coli bacteria.

(RB) *Ring Bologna & Potato Soup*

I was taught to make potato soup the old-fashioned way by a neighbor who followed no recipe. I have evolved the soup to its current state and taken this opportunity to write it down for you. Have fun and remember you really can't go wrong whatever you add to it.

Serves: 8+

1 ring bologna cut into bite-sized chunks

4 cups potatoes, cut into bite-sized chunks

1 cup of baby carrots, halved

water to cover

1 cup cheddar cheese, shredded

milk

Place potatoes and carrots into large stockpot and cover with water so it is about an inch or 2 over the top of the potatoes and carrots. Bring to a boil, then simmer until soft, about 20 minutes. In a blender, place half of the potatoes, all of the carrots and some of the cooking water and liquefy. Pour mixture back into the stockpot with remaining potatoes. Mixture will be orange and thick. Add cheese and cook over medium heat until melted. Add milk to achieve desired consistency.

(Stk) (Rst) *Basic Stew*

This recipe is simple, or should I say simply delicious. If you like to taste the true flavors of venison and vegetables, this recipe will be a favorite.

Serves: 4-6

1-1/2 pounds venison, cubed

1 14 oz can diced tomatoes

1 cup baby carrots, halved

1 medium onion, sliced

4 medium potatoes, peeled and chunked

2 cups water, divided

1/4 cup flour

Preheat oven to 325 degrees.
Place all ingredients except flour and 1 cup of the water in covered roasting pan and bake for 2-1/2 to 3 hours. I usually add the second cup of water after about 2 hours of cooking. Remove some stew drippings and add flour to make a loose paste. Stir into stew and heat while stirring over medium stove burner until sauce thickens.

CLEANLINESS IS KEY
Most venison-related illnesses do not come from the meat itself; they come from secondary contamination from uncleanly processing facilities. To ensure your meat is safe, be diligent to keep all processing knives, utensils and work areas clean. Wash knives and utensils in hot, soapy water and dry thoroughly with a clean towel. Keep work areas bacteria-free by washing them down frequently with a water-bleach solution.

Stk Rst *Catawba Chowder*

What isn't in this chowder? This is a chunky, rich concoction where you count the flavors not the calories.

Serves: 6

1 cup venison, diced
2 tablespoons vegetable oil
2 cups baby carrots, sliced
1 sweet red pepper, diced
1/2 cup red onion, chopped
1 14 oz can diced tomatoes, drained
1 15 oz can whole kernel corn, drained
2 cups russet potatoes, cubed

32 oz beef broth
salt & pepper to taste
1 15 oz can black beans, rinsed and drained
1 teaspoon thyme
2 tablespoons butter
3 tablespoons flour
2 cups half 'n half

In large stockpot, add vegetables and broth and simmer for 90 minutes. In skillet, brown meat in vegetable oil and drain fat. Add meat, beans and seasonings and cook for an additional 50 minutes. Make a rue in a small saucepan with the butter and flour, and when lightly brown, stir into the chowder. When blended together, add half 'n half and continue to cook until thickened.

Stk Rst *Gardener's Stovetop Stew*

This quick-prep stew cooks on your stovetop, allowing you time to sit down and take a break while still providing a hot, nutritious meal for your family and friends.

Serves: 4

1-1/2 pounds venison, cubed
2 tablespoons vegetable oil
1 14 oz can diced tomatoes with juice
2-1/4 cup water

1 cup baby carrots, cut into thirds
16 white pearl onions
3 russet potatoes, cut into chunks
1/4 teaspoon thyme

In skillet, brown meat in vegetable oil and drain fat. Add tomatoes with juice and water. Cover and simmer for 60 minutes. Add vegetables, thyme and additional water if needed, then cook for an additional 50 minutes, stirring occasionally. Uncover and continue cooking, allowing the sauce to reduce and thicken if needed.

THE SECRET TO SUPER SAUSAGE

A deer's neck, shoulder and leg meat are prime sources of sausage meat. The key to good venison sausage, however, is to start with 100 percent lean scraps. This means a lot of tedious work with the trimming knife. Unlike pork and beef, venison tallow will ruin an otherwise excellent batch of sausage. When trimming tallow from sausage meat, clean your knife frequently to prevent smearing tallow remnants onto clean cuts of meat.

Stk Rst *Pot O' Gold Stew*

We like to use a great Wisconsin beer in this recipe. The rich flavor really complements the natural flavors of the veggies and meat.

Serves: 6-8

2 pounds venison, cubed
2 tablespoons vegetable oil
4 cloves garlic, minced
7 cups beef broth
1 bottle creamy dark lager beer
2 tablespoons tomato paste
1 tablespoon brown sugar
1 tablespoon oregano

1-1/2 tablespoons Worcestershire sauce
16 white pearl onions
7 cups russet potatoes, chunked
2 cups baby carrots, halved
1/4 cup flour
1/4 cup water

In stockpot, brown venison in oil. Add garlic and sauté until soft but not brown. Add broth, beer, tomato paste, brown sugar, oregano and Worcestershire sauce. Boil and then reduce heat to simmer for 60 minutes, stirring occasionally. Add vegetables and then cook for an additional 60 minutes, continuing to stir occasionally until vegetables are tender. Mix water and flour in glass measuring cup and add to stew. Continue cooking, mixing until thickened.

Stk Rst *Scandinavian Stew*

The only thing you need to cut up in this stew is the star of the recipe, the venison. It doesn't get much easier to put comfort food on the table.

Serves: 4

1-1/2 pounds venison, cubed
2 tablespoons vegetable oil
2-1/4 cup water
1 10-3/4 oz can condensed
   cream of mushroom soup

1 tablespoon red wine vinegar
1/4 teaspoon cinnamon
16 white pearl onions
1 4 oz can chunky Portabella
   mushrooms, drained

In large skillet, brown meat in vegetable oil and drain fat. Add all ingredients except mushrooms and onions. Cover and simmer for 90 minutes. Add onions and mushrooms, then cover and cook for an additional 40 minutes, stirring occasionally. Uncover and continue cooking, allowing the sauce to reduce and thicken if needed.

USE THE THREE-DAY RULE

Frozen fat-free venison has an extremely long shelf life. Some processors say up to 18 months. In fact, frozen venison never really spoils; it just loses its quality. Fresh venison is another story. Whether you are dealing with fresh tenderloins from an opening-day buck or the thawed flank steaks from last year's doe, venison should never be kept for more than three days in a refrigerator.

Rst *Snowstorm Stew*

This slow cook, great aroma, great taste stew can't be beat on a day when you are snowbound. Make some homemade bread, rolls or biscuits to go with it.

Serves: 4-6

2 pounds, venison, cubed
1 cup baby carrots, halved
1 10-1/4 oz can diced tomatoes
1 bay leaf
16 white pearl onions

3 russet potatoes, cut into
 bite-sized chunks
1 cup red cooking wine
1 6 oz can mushrooms, drained
1 package frozen beans

Preheat oven to 275 degrees.
In large casserole, place venison, carrots, tomatoes, bay leaf, onions, potatoes and 3/4 cup wine. Cover and bake for 4 hours. Add beans, mushrooms, onions, remaining red cooking wine and cook for an additional 60 minutes, adding additional water as needed to prevent scorching.

Rst *Stroganoff Stew*

The paprika results in a rich, caramel-colored dish that tastes so great it will leave you wanting seconds.

Serves: 6

2 pounds venison, cubed
2 tablespoons vegetable oil
2 cans 10-3/4 oz can condensed
 cream of mushroom soup
1/2 cup sour cream
1/2 cup water

1-1/2 teaspoons paprika
pepper
1 cup baby carrots, halved
16 white pearl onions
egg noodles, prepared

In skillet, brown meat in vegetable oil and drain fat. Add all ingredients except carrots and onions. Cover and simmer for 90 minutes. Add carrots after 60 minutes has passed. Add onions 30 minutes later, then cook for an additional 50 minutes, stirring occasionally. Uncover and continue cooking, allowing the sauce to reduce and thicken if needed. Serve over noodles.

RAINY DAY JERKY TIPS
   To make jerky from frozen venison, be sure to first thaw the meat in the refrigerator. Do not leave it out on the kitchen counter. End quality and overall safety require a slow thaw so ice crystals do not rupture and further moisture the meat fibers. Marinades (to add flavor) should also be done at refrigerator temperatures for one to two days. After heating the meat to an internal temperature of 165 degrees (a microwave oven will suffice), dry the jerky in a food dehydrator at a temperature of 130 to 140 degrees.

Stk Rst *Vegetable Soup*

Vegetable soup is great to serve alongside grilled Muenster cheese sandwiches. If you use frozen beans, cook them in the microwave until they are warm. That way, when you add them to the pot, they won't cool your soup.

Serves: 10

1-1/2 pounds venison, cubed
32 oz beef broth
6 cups water
1 large onion, chopped
3 cloves garlic, diced
1 teaspoon salt
dash pepper
1 medium red onion, sliced

1-1/2 cups potatoes, peeled
  and diced
1 cup baby carrots, cut in thirds
1/2 cup green bean pieces, 1/2" long
  (frozen work great)
1 14 oz. can diced tomatoes
1/2 teaspoon oregano
1 cup uncooked elbow macaroni

In a covered 6-quart stockpot, simmer venison, broth, chopped onion, garlic, salt, pepper and water for 1 hour. Add sliced onion, potatoes, carrots, beans and tomatoes with juice and oregano. Cook covered for another 25 minutes, then check for vegetable tenderness. If tender, add macaroni and cook an additional 12 minutes. If not yet tender, cook an additional 30 minutes before adding the macaroni and completing the recipe.

Top 10 Shortcut Items

1. Peeled and washed baby carrots cut up in chunks or used whole
2. Frozen potatoes
3. Refrigerated pie crust
4. Frozen ready-to-use onion pearls
5. Toast for breadcrumbs or cheddar-cheese-flavored crackers
6. Jarred, minced garlic
7. Use as few utensils as possible: know your equivalents and choose recipes that are consistent in quantities
8. Use silicone pad or rubber jar opener to roll skin off of garlic
9. Microwave limes whole for 10-15 seconds on high and then press and roll on the counter to make juicing it easier
10. Clean up as you cook

UP OR DOWN?

Some hunters prefer to hang a deer head up, but the head-down position remains better for several reasons. First, it allows heat to rise freely from the chest cavity. Second, it makes it easier to skin the head out, an important consideration if the deer is a trophy. Finally, it reduces the amount of hair you get on the meat while skinning.

Chapter 4:

Sweet & Savory

Chp *Apricot-Glazed Venison Chops*

It doesn't get much easier than five ingredients, a skillet, a spoon and a bowl. This dish has a mild flavor that still allows you to taste the meat rather than drowning it out with overly sweet flavors.

Serves: 4

4 venison chops
1/3 cup apricot preserves
1/3 cup water

1/2 teaspoon ground ginger
2 tablespoons vegetable oil

In skillet, brown chops for 5 minutes on each side in vegetable oil. In small bowl, mix preserves, water and ginger. Baste chops, add sauce to pan, cover and continue cooking an additional 20 minutes or until cooked through.

Top 5 Tips to a Great Roast:

1. The slower and longer the more tender. My favorite temperature to cook a roast at is 275 degrees. It takes 2 hours plus or minus depending on the size of the roast and how well done you like it.

2. Cook to 172-degrees Fahrenheit at the most.

3. Use a cooking thermometer and really monitor the temperature of your roast. Roasts do not usually come with a weight on them, so there is a lot of variance in shape and size. This means cooking times can vary widely. The only way not to waste a hard-earned roast is with a thermometer.

4. Neck roast can be used, but take the meat off the bones. The tallow can be overwhelming, but the meat is really tender.

5. Make sure to let your roast rest 10-15 minutes before you slice it so the moisture is wicked up into the meat and the meat has cooled enough to not fall apart as readily when cut unless a shredded sandwich is what you are after.

SLOW AND STEADY

Venison handling techniques in the field, on the butcher table and in the kitchen all benefit from slow and steady procedures. This is especially true in the kitchen. Frozen venison should be allowed to thaw slowly to prevent toughness. Venison roasts and stew meat should also be cooked slowly, covered, to prevent meat from getting tough and dried out.

⒞ *Candied Orange Chops*

These chops have a vibrant, sweet orange flavor. You might want to hold back 1/4 cup of the Basic Orange Sauce to drizzle over the plated chops before serving.

Serves: 4

6 boneless venison chops, butterflied	2 tablespoons fresh parsley
1 tablespoon dried orange peel	2 tablespoons butter
3/4 cup orange juice	1-1/4 cups dried bread crumbs
3 tablespoons sugar	1/2 teaspoon thyme
1/4 cup red onion, diced	1/2 teaspoon salt
	2 tablespoons vegetable oil

Preheat oven to 350 degrees.

In medium saucepan, combine orange juice, orange peel and sugar to create a glaze, and stir until mixture boils. Once sauce is boiling, reduce heat and simmer for 5 minutes, stirring as needed, then set aside to cool. In skillet, sauté onion and parsley in butter until soft but not brown. Add bread crumbs, thyme, salt and cooled sauce to skillet and mix with orange glaze. Remove stuffing from skillet, add oil and brown chops 3 minutes on each side. Remove chops from pan and return stuffing to skillet. Place chops on top and pour Basic Orange Sauce over the top, cover and cook 5 additional minutes.

Basic Orange Sauce

2 tablespoons butter	1 cup water
2 tablespoons flour	2 tablespoons orange juice

In saucepan, melt butter and stir in flour until slightly browned. Add water and orange juice all at once. Cook, stirring constantly until thick and bubbly. Use to top chops as directed above.

⒞ *Citrus-Glazed Chops*

The combination of apricot, orange and lime work great together. There is enough sweetness to remove the acidity from the lime. See if your friends can guess the surprise ingredient in this dish (lime).

Serves: 4

4 venison chops	3 tablespoons apricot preserves
1 tablespoon extra virgin olive oil	1/2 small lime, juiced
1/4 cup orange juice	1 tablespoon red wine vinegar
3 tablespoons brown sugar	

In skillet, brown chops in olive oil for 3 minutes on each side. In small bowl, mix orange juice, preserves, lime, vinegar and brown sugar. Baste chops, add sauce to pan, cover and continue cooking an additional 10 minutes or until cooked through.

Chp *Dijon & Pecan Chops*

When making this dish, measure your honey after the oil and your measuring cup won't be sticky. This is my favorite chop recipe. Remember to chop your pecans very finely, as they will be part of the breading. If they are too large, they will fall off the chops.

Serves: 4

4 boneless venison chops, pounded
   to 1/4" thick
1 tablespoon Dijon mustard
1/4 cup honey
1/4 cup vegetable oil
1/4 cup soy sauce
2 tablespoons white wine vinegar

1 small onion, chopped
4 cloves garlic, crushed
1/4 teaspoon ground ginger
3/4 cup pecans, chopped very fine
1 tablespoon dried parsley
1/2 cup dry bread crumbs
2 tablespoons vegetable oil

In quart-size plastic bag, add mustard, honey, vegetable oil, soy sauce, vinegar, onion, garlic and ginger. Place venison in bag and marinate overnight. Remove chops and discard marinade. In shallow dish, combine pecans, parsley and bread crumbs. Dredge venison chops in coating. In large skillet, heat oil and add venison chops. Cook 15-20 minutes or until done, turning during cooking time. Spread remaining toasted nuts from the skillet over the serving plate.

Chp *High-Five Venison Chops*

These easy-prep chops cook up great on the grill. We eat them all summer. The acidity in the pineapple really helps soften up the chops.

Serves: 4

4 venison chops
1/4 cup teriyaki sauce
2 cloves garlic, crushed

1 8 oz can crushed pineapple
   with juice
1/2 small onion, diced

Place marinade ingredients in a quart-size plastic bag. Add chops and let sit overnight. Place on grill and cook for 10-15 minutes, turning halfway through cooking time.

KEEP IT HOT

Temperature is the key to tasty venison steaks, chops roasts and stews. All of these meals should be prepared, kept and served hot. Keeping your venison at its ultimate eating temperature without burning it prevents the waxy taste that some folks call "gamey." The waxy taste comes from tallow residue on the meat. This residue is more apparent when meat is allowed to cool before it is consumed.

(Grd) *Easy Chair Meatloaf*

A favorite fall meatloaf that tastes great alongside a baked potato and cooked acorn squash. It cooks for an hour, so there is plenty of time to sit down and catch your breath in your favorite chair. The Granny Smith apples are firmer when cooked than many other apples.

Serves: 8

2 pounds venison, ground
1 large onion, diced
2 tablespoons butter
1-1/2 cups soft bread crumbs
2 cups Granny Smith apples, peeled,
  cored and chopped
3 eggs, beaten

1 tablespoon dried parsley
pepper
1 teaspoon salt
1/4 teaspoon allspice
1 tablespoon prepared mustard
1/4 cup ketchup
1 tablespoon brown sugar

Preheat oven to 350 degrees.
In skillet, cook onion in butter until soft. Allow to cool and then in large bowl, combine all ingredients. Form into a loaf and place on a cookie sheet. Bake for 1 hour or until cooked through. Allow loaf to rest for 15 minutes before slicing.

(Grd) *Teriyaki Burgers*

Tapioca? Well, it doesn't change the flavor of the burger, and it goes a long way to help hold the meat together when grilling. Venison is a very lean meat, and it needs a little help with moisture so it doesn't fall apart when cooking. I first learned to use tapioca from an old chili recipe that incorporated it as a thickening agent.

Serves: 4

1 pound venison, ground
1 tablespoon tapioca
1/4 cup teriyaki sauce

1/4 cup scallions, sliced
1/4 cup sweet green pepper, minced
hamburger buns

Mix the first five ingredients and let stand for 10 minutes. Press into patties and cook in skillet or on grill until cooked through.
Place patties onto buns.

LIGHTEN YOUR LOAD
Field dressing ("gutting") a deer is extremely important step in the handling of venison. It not only helps rid the body cavity of acids and bacteria, it helps lighten your load back to camp. The average deer will weigh up to 20 percent less after it has been field dressed. In the case of a mature buck, that could mean 40 to 50 pounds. So save your back, and dress your deer before dragging it out of the woods!

(Rst) *Bengi Ridge Roast*

A Coffee Lake Hunting Club staple, the sweet and sour flavors work well together to create a flavorful roast.

Serves: 6

2 pounds venison roast
1-1/4 cup water
1/4 cup vegetable oil
1/4 cup soy sauce
1/4 cup honey

1/4 cup cider vinegar
4 cloves garlic, crushed
1/2 tsp dry ginger
1/2 tsp onion powder

Preheat oven to 325 degrees when ready to bake.
In gallon-size plastic bag, add all ingredients except water and roast. Reserve 1/4 cup of sauce for basting. Place roast in bag and marinate overnight. Place roast in roasting pan, add water, cover and roast for 1-1/2 hours, basting with reserved marinade. Return uncovered to oven and bake for an additional 30 minutes, basting every 10 minutes until desired doneness is reached.

(Rst) *Sweet & Sour Roast*

We like the flavor of this roast because it is not overly sweet and sticky. Venison roasts can be tricky to cook.

Serves: 6

2 pounds venison roast
1 cup beef broth
1 cup onion, sliced
1-1/4 cups water
1 tablespoon soy sauce

2 tablespoons cider vinegar
2 tablespoons brown sugar
1 teaspoon garlic powder
1 teaspoon ground ginger

Preheat oven to 325 degrees.
Place venison in roasting pan, add water and beef broth and roast for 30 minutes. Mix remaining ingredients and baste roast. Return uncovered to oven and bake for an additional 30-60 minutes, basting every 10 minutes until desired doneness is reached.

WEIGHT VARIANCES BY REGION
The typical Northern white-tailed fawn, which includes "button bucks," weighs about 55 to 75 pounds field dressed in November. Healthy doe fawns weigh anywhere from 45 to 65 pounds field dressed. Southern fawns weigh much less — sometimes less than 30 pounds field dressed. De-boned meat yields of fawns range from 30+ pounds in the North to 15 to 20 pounds in the South.

(Stk) *Ginger & Pineapple Kabobs*

This recipe has a milder flavor than the other kabob recipes in this book.

Serves: 6

1-1/2 pounds venison steak, cubed
1/4 cup honey
1 tablespoon ground ginger
3/4 cup vegetable oil
1/4 cup soy sauce
2 tablespoons Worcestershire sauce
1/4 cup red wine vinegar

1 can pineapple chunks with juice
   reserved
4 cloves garlic, crushed
2 large onions, wedged
2 sweet red peppers, chunked
wooden skewers, soaked

In quart-size plastic bag, add all ingredients except venison, pineapple, onions and peppers. Add 2 tablespoons of pineapple juice. Mix and reserve 1/2 cup for basting. Add venison, peppers and onions and marinate overnight. Remove venison, peppers and onions. Place on skewers, alternating with pineapple chunks and grill 10 minutes, basting with reserved marinade.

(Stk) *Sesame Stir-Fry*

Who doesn't love the great taste and ease of a stir-fry at the end of the day? The sesame seeds are a great addition to this dish.

Serves: 4

1-1/2 pounds venison steak, sliced
   into thin strips
2 tablespoons brown sugar
2 tablespoons vegetable oil
2 tablespoons soy sauce

1/4 cup scallions
3 cloves garlic, minced
1 tablespoon sesame seeds
1 tablespoon butter
rice, prepared

In large bowl, place all ingredients except butter and rice. Mix and let stand for 20 minutes. In large skillet, melt butter and add venison and marinade. Cook until meat is cooked through and serve over prepared rice.

KEEP THEM TENDER

For the ultimate opening-day celebration, immediately remove your deer's inside tenderloins after getting the deer back to camp. The inside tenderloins are the most delectable cut of venison. They hug the rear portion of the deer's spine on the inside of the stomach cavity. For an appetizer, wash the tenderloin in cold water and pat dry with toweling. Slice cross-grain into medallion-sized pieces and pan fry in butter with onions and garlic. Serve with buttered toast and a cold beverage.

Sesame Venison

This is as simple and flavorful as it gets. I often thaw a 2-pack of steaks and use one for this recipe and the other one for kabobs.

Serves: 4

1 pound venison steak, sliced into
  thin strips
2 tablespoons brown sugar
3 tablespoons vegetable oil, divided
2 tablespoons soy sauce

dash pepper
1/4 cup onion, diced
3 cloves garlic, minced
1 tablespoon sesame seeds
rice, prepared

In medium bowl, combine sugar, 2 tablespoons oil, soy sauce, garlic, onion, pepper and sesame seeds. Add beef slices and coat. Let sit for 20 minutes. In large skillet, heat 1 tablespoon oil. Add venison and marinade and cook until venison is done. Serve over prepared rice.

 Sesame-Orange Kabobs

Hoisin sauce is found with the Oriental sauces in most supermarkets. It adds a sweet, fruity and tomato-based flavor to the kabobs. The rice vinegar is a nice complement with its mild sweetness.

Serves: 6

1-1/2 pounds venison steak, cubed
1/2 cup hoisin sauce
1/2 cup ketchup
1/4 cup seasoned rice vinegar
1/4 cup vegetable oil
1/4 cup orange juice

1 tablespoon sesame seeds
1 teaspoon garlic powder
1 medium zucchini, halved and
  chunked
wooden skewers, soaked

In quart-size plastic bag, add all ingredients except venison and zucchini. Mix and reserve 1/2 cup for basting. Place venison in bag and marinate overnight. Remove venison, discard marinade and place meat on skewers, alternating with zucchini. Grill 10 to 15 minutes, basting with reserved marinade.

SKIN, BONES AND MORE
   Hunters often brag about the field dressed weights of their bucks, but have you ever wondered how much of that weight is, well, waste? According to a study by the Pennsylvania State University Department of Animal Science, a 180-pound buck (live weight) would carry 16.2 pounds of hide, 21.06 pounds of bones and nine pounds of blood.

Stk *Steak & Veggie Kabobs*

The flavor of this marinade is very good. Its sweetness really penetrates the meat. In fact, the first time my kids ate this for dinner they didn't even realize it was venison they were eating.

Serves: 10

1 pound venison steak, cubed
20 cherry tomatoes
3 large sweet peppers, seeds
  removed and chunked

2 small zucchini, sliced
1 large onion, wedged
skewers, metal or soaked wood
Marinade (see below)

Place marinade ingredients in a quart-size bag, reserve a little for basting, add cubed venison and let sit overnight. Alternate meat and veggies on skewers. Grill until done.

Marinade
1/4 cup olive oil
1/4 cup soy sauce

1/4 cup brown sugar, packed
1 teaspoon garlic powder

Stk *Veni Chop Suey*

This dish is a fast prep, fast cook delight of fabulous flavor and texture. If you like Oriental takeout, you will like this dish made much more economically at home.

Serves: 4

1 pound venison steak, sliced into
  thin strips
2 tablespoons vegetable oil
1 can sliced mushrooms, drained
1/2 cup water

1 tablespoon soy sauce
1 cup sweet green pepper, chopped
1 14 oz can diced tomatoes
1/2 cup scallions, sliced
1 cup celery, diced

In skillet, brown venison steak slices in oil. Add remaining ingredients, cover and simmer for 20 minutes or until meat is tender.

OFF THE CHARTS

For decades, some hunters have relied on chest-girth charts to estimate live weights of deer. Unfortunately, such charts are often inaccurate because — among other things — they don't account for fluctuations in the body sizes of bucks before and after the rut. Therefore, most professional biologists put no stock in any weight estimates based on chest-girth measurements.

Chapter 5:
Tomato-Based

Chp *Tomato-Topped Chops*

Balsamic vinegar adds great flavor to both the tomatoes and meat in this dish.

Serves: 6

6 boneless venison chops
vegetable oil
water

14 oz can of diced tomatoes,
   juice drained
1/4 cup balsamic vinegar

Place oil in skillet and brown chops in oil for 5 minutes on each side. Add water until a depth of 1 inch is reached in skillet. Cover and cook for an additional 10 minutes. In small bowl, combine tomatoes and vinegar. Place on top of chops and re-cover to cook for an additional 10 minutes.

Grd *Barbeque Meatloaf*

This meatloaf is very moist and goes great with traditional sides of green beans and buttered mashed potatoes.

Serves: 6

1 pound venison, ground
1 medium onion, minced
1-1/2 tablespoons butter
1 egg

1/2 cup soft bread crumbs
1/2 cup tomato sauce
1 teaspoon salt
1/4 teaspoon pepper

Preheat oven to 350 degrees.
Melt butter in skillet. Add onion and cook until softened. Combine with other ingredients in large bowl. Mix well and form into loaf. Bake in large, greased loaf pan for 40 minutes. Remove and add half of sauce to coat, and return to oven for an additional 10 minutes. Take out and baste with additional sauce and put back in oven for an additional 10 minutes.

Barbecue Sauce
1-1/2 cups tomato sauce
1/2 cup water
2-1/2 tablespoons Worcestershire
   sauce

2 tablespoons prepared mustard
3 tablespoons brown sugar
2 tablespoons cider vinegar

Heat all ingredients in saucepan over medium heat, stirring until well blended. Use on meatloaf as described above.

(Grd) *Buck Hunter's Bake*

A deer camp staple in our family, this recipe full of meat, potatoes and corn tastes great on a crisp fall night.

Serves: 6

1 pound venison, ground
3 cups instant potato flakes
16 oz sour cream
1/2 cup water
1/4 cup onion, chopped
1 15 oz can tomato sauce
1 15 oz can whole kernel corn,
    drained

1/2 cup water
1 teaspoon garlic powder
1 tablespoon brown sugar
1 teaspoon ground cumin
1/2 teaspoon salt
pepper
1 cup cheddar cheese, shredded

Preheat oven to 350 degrees.
In large casserole, mix potato flakes, sour cream, garlic powder and 1/2 cup water to create a crumbly mixture. Press firmly into bottom of pan to form crust. In skillet, brown venison and onion, drain fat. Add 1/2 cup water and remaining ingredients except cheese. Layer the venison mixture over the potato mixture in baking pan. Cover the top with cheese. Bake for 25-30 minutes.

(Grd) *Burger Pie*

The kids love to eat this pie for dinner. It is so simple to prepare that they are able to help make it. They love pressing the dough into the pie plate.

Serves: 8

1 pound venison, ground
1/4 cup onion, minced
1 teaspoon salt
pepper
1/2 teaspoon dried basil
1/2 teaspoon garlic powder

1/4 teaspoon dried oregano
1 6 oz can tomato paste
1 can refrigerated crescent roll
    dough
1-1/2 cups mozzarella cheese,
    shredded

Preheat oven to 375 degrees.
In skillet, brown ground venison and onion, drain off fat. Cool and mix with remaining ingredients except dough and cheese in a large mixing bowl. Unroll and separate dough into triangles. Place into a 9-inch pie plate and press together to make a crust. Add meat mixture and bake for 15 minutes. Remove from oven and top with shredded cheese. Return to oven for an additional 15 minutes. Tent with aluminum foil if the crust starts to become overly brown.

Cranberry Joes

Cinnamon helps enhance the sweet tones of this dish. My kids always ask for second helpings.

Serves: 6

1 pound venison, ground	1/2 teaspoon salt
1/2 cup celery, chopped	1 teaspoon chili powder
1/2 cup onion, chopped	1/2 teaspoon cinnamon
1 8 oz can jellied cranberry sauce	hamburger buns
1 10-3/4 oz can condensed tomato soup	

In skillet, brown venison, celery and onion until meat is brown and onions soft. Remove fat and add soup and cranberry sauce. Stir until mixed and add salt, cinnamon and chili powder. Simmer 20-30 minutes uncovered and serve over buns.

 Cranberry Meatballs

The tang of the cranberries and heat from the taco sauce work well with the sweet elements in this dish. Remember, the meatballs are small, so chop the onions small so they incorporate well into the meat. Make these a day ahead of your party and reheat for the best flavor.

Serves: 15-20

2 pounds venison, ground	1 tablespoon dried parsley flakes
2 eggs, slightly beaten	1/4 cup onion, minced
1 cup dry bread crumbs	1/4 teaspoon salt
1/3 cup ketchup	1/8 teaspoon pepper
2-1/2 tablespoons soy sauce	1 teaspoon red pepper flakes

Preheat oven to 350 degrees.
In large mixing bowl, combine all meatball ingredients and mix just until blended. Form into 1-inch meatballs and place on cookie sheets. Bake for 25 minutes. Remove when cooked through and drain on paper towels. Prepare sauce and add meatballs to saucepan until they are heated through.

Cranberry Sauce

1 16 oz can jellied cranberry sauce	1 tablespoon lemon juice
1 8 oz bottle mild taco sauce	1 tablespoon hoisin sauce
3 tablespoons brown sugar	

In a large saucepan, combine all sauce ingredients over medium-low heat. Stir constantly until melted and add cooked meatballs (see above).

Grd *Goulash*

Goulash is one of my favorite quick-fix meals to cook and eat after hunting in the fall. Add a roll and salad, and dinner is served.

Serves: 6

1 pound venison, ground
1 teaspoon garlic powder
1 teaspoon dried oregano
pepper

1/4 cup onion
2 14-1/4 oz cans stewed tomatoes
1-1/2 cups elbow noodles

Cook elbow noodles according to package directions. In skillet, brown ground venison and onion, drain fat and stir in oregano, pepper, garlic and cans of stewed tomatoes. Combine noodles with other ingredients in skillet. Warm and serve.

Grd *Hearty Casserole*

Make sure to slice the potatoes thinly so they cook through. This casserole is based on the hobo packs we used to make in foil and grill when camping.

Serves: 6

1 pound venison, ground
1 cup onion, minced
1 14 oz can diced tomatoes with
   juice
1 tablespoon Worcestershire sauce
1 teaspoon salt
1 teaspoon garlic powder

1 teaspoon dried basil
2 cups potatoes, thinly sliced
   like chips
1 can corn
1 can green beans
1-1/2 cups cheddar cheese,
   shredded

Preheat oven to 375 degrees.
Brown venison in skillet and drain fat. Place all ingredients except cheese in large mixing bowl. Blend and transfer into a greased 3-quart casserole. Cover and bake for 45 minutes. Remove from oven and add cheese to top. Cook for an additional 30 minutes until cheese in nicely browned.

RUT PHASE AFFECTS MEAT YIELD
A buck's condition plays a large role in how much boneless venison it will yield. For example, a buck killed during the peak of November's rut will often have the physique of a body builder. Although its neck will be swollen and shoulders muscled, its hips and back will appear nearly fat-free. The same buck might field dress 10 pounds more if it had been killed in late September or early October.

(Grd) *Italian Casserole*

Push down on the spinach in a strainer with paper towels to really get the moisture out. It will keep your casserole from being watery.

Serves: 6

1 pound venison, ground
2 10 oz packages frozen spinach,
  cooked and drained
16 oz cottage cheese
2 8 oz cans tomato sauce
1/2 cup chopped onion, chopped
1 tablespoon dried parsley lakes

1/2 teaspoon dried oregano
1/2 teaspoon dried basil
1 teaspoon garlic powder
1 tablespoon brown sugar
1/2 teaspoon salt
pepper
1 cup mozzarella cheese, shredded

Preheat oven to 375 degrees.
In skillet, brown venison and onions, drain fat. Stir in tomato sauce, basil, oregano, parsley, garlic powder, brown sugar, salt and pepper. Simmer uncovered for 10 minutes, occasionally stirring to prevent scorching. In a large bowl, combine spinach and cottage cheese. Spoon spinach mixture around edges of 13-inch x 9-inch baking dish. Place venison mixture in middle. Place mozzarella over the top and bake for 20-25 minutes.

(Grd) *Lasagna with Venison*

Paired with garlic bread and a salad, bake this recipe on Sunday and reheat for an easy middle-of-the week meal.

Serves: 12

1 pound venison, ground, cooked
  and drained
1/2 box lasagna noodles, cooked
  per package instructions
4 cups shredded mozzarella cheese
1/4 cup Parmesan cheese

1 15 oz container ricotta cheese
1 teaspoon garlic powder
1 tablespoon dried parsley
2 eggs, slightly beaten
2 26 oz jars spaghetti sauce

Preheat oven to 375 degrees.
Spray a 13-inch x 9-inch dish with cooking spray. In a large bowl, combine eggs, Parmesan, ricotta, garlic and parsley and 3 cups of mozzarella cheese. Spread 1/3 jar of spaghetti sauce in bottom of pan. Place 3-4 noodles across the pan's bottom. Spread a layer of cheese mixture over that, then a layer of meat followed by a layer of sauce. Repeat layers covering the final layer with remaining cup of mozzarella cheese. Cover with foil and bake for 30 minutes. Bake an additional 10 minutes with the foil off to slightly brown the cheese. Let stand 15 minutes before serving.

Grd M.A.'s Meatballs & Spaghetti

I love to make these ahead and keep them in the freezer for future use. I put a little sauce over them and heat them in the microwave.

Makes: 24 meatballs

1-1/2 pound venison, ground
1 egg, beaten slightly
3/4 cup dry bread crumbs
1/3 cup milk
1-1/2 teaspoons Worcestershire
   sauce

1/4 cup onion, finely minced
1/4 teaspoon salt
1/4 teaspoon garlic powder
dash of pepper
prepared spaghetti noodles
1 jar prepared spaghetti sauce

Preheat oven to 350 degrees.

In a large bowl, combine all ingredients except venison noodles and sauce. Add the venison to the other ingredients mixing only until blended. Shape into meatballs and place on baking sheets. Bake for 30 minutes or until no longer pink in middle. Heat spaghetti sauce, serve over meatball-topped pasta.

Meatballs not used can be cooled, drained on paper towels, and placed in a freezer bag. They might remain frozen for up to six months.

Grd Mini Loaves

The night before making this dish, I prep the string cheese and mix the seasonings and parsley together. I also mix the sauce ahead of time, making this meal fast to pull together during the work week.

Serves: 6

1 pound venison, ground
1 egg, slightly beaten
1 cup dry bread crumbs
1/4 cup milk
1/2 teaspoon onion powder

1/2 teaspoon garlic powder
1 teaspoon dried parsley flakes
pepper
3 sticks of mozzarella string cheese
   cut in half (approx 2-3 inches long)

In large mixing bowl, mix egg, bread crumbs, milk and seasonings. Add ground venison and mix only until blended. Divide meat into six equal portions and encase string cheese logs in the middle of each loaf. Place loaves into large skillet. Add sauce, cover and bring to a boil. Simmer until completely cooked, about 20 minutes.

Meatloaf Sauce

30 oz tomato sauce
1 teaspoon onion powder
1/2 teaspoon dried basil
1/2 teaspoon dried oregano

1 teaspoon garlic powder
1 tablespoon dried parsley flakes
pepper

Mix sauce ingredients in bowl. Cover meatloaves with sauce and pour rest of sauce into skillet (see above).

(Grd) *Prickly Porcupine Meatballs*

You might quickly find yourself hooked on this kid favorite. My little ones love the taste just as much as the name.

Serves: 4

1 pound venison, ground
3 pieces of string cheese sliced
   into 5 segments each
1 10-3/4 oz can condensed
   tomato soup
1 cup prepared rice
1 egg, beaten slightly

1/3 cup onion, finely chopped
1/2 teaspoon salt
1 teaspoon garlic powder
2 tablespoons vegetable oil
3/4 cup water
1 teaspoon prepared mustard

Put venison, egg, onion, rice and salt in a medium bowl. Add 1/4 cup soup. Shape into 15 meatballs with string cheese in the middle. In skillet, heat the oil, then brown the meatballs. Drain the fat off. In bowl, add mustard, remaining soup, garlic and water, then add to skillet. Cover and simmer 20 minutes or until done. Stir occasionally.

(Grd) *Salsa Meatball Tortilla Wraps*

These sandwiches are fun to make with the kids. We wrap the meatballs and salsa in a warm tortilla along with some lettuce and sour cream.

Serves: 4

2 pounds venison, ground
2 eggs, slightly beaten
3/4 cup dry bread crumbs
1/2 cup milk
1 package taco seasoning mix
2 jars salsa

2/3 cup mild cheddar cheese,
   shredded
warm tortillas
lettuce
sour cream

Preheat oven to 350 degrees.
Mix venison, eggs, bread crumbs, milk and taco seasoning in large bowl. Form meatballs and place on baking sheet. Cook for 20 minutes, then remove and allow to cool. Spray a baking dish with nonstick spray and spread one jar of salsa on bottom. Put meatballs into dish and pour remaining jar of salsa over the top. Bake for 15 minutes, then remove and cover top with cheese. Cook an additional 5 minutes or until cheese has melted. Place meatballs in tortillas and top with lettuce and sour cream.

KEEP YOUR EDGE
   Venison processing becomes much easier, even fun, when you use quality knives. However, the best knife is useless if you don't also invest in a sharpening steel or set of stones.

Saucy Diner Loaf

A comfort food favorite in my family and also my top meatloaf pick.

Serves: 5-6

1-1/2 pounds venison, ground
1 cup bread crumbs
3/4 cup milk
1/4 cup onion, finely minced
1/4 cup Balsamic vinegar
1/2 cup Parmesan cheese

1 egg, slightly beaten
1 teaspoon salt
1/4 teaspoon pepper
1/4 teaspoon basil
1 8 oz can tomato sauce
4 slices mozzarella cheese

Preheat oven to 350 degrees.

In large bowl, combine all ingredients except tomato sauce and mozzarella cheese. Mix gently with fingertips. Shape loaf in 9-1/4-inch x 5-1/4-inch loaf pan and bake. Remove from oven after 90 minutes. Drain fat, pour on the tomato sauce and place back in oven for 30 minutes. Remove from oven and place the cheese on top. Put back in the oven for about 10 minutes until cheese is melted.

Sloppy Joes

Aromatic cumin adds a new depth of flavor to this traditional family dinner favorite.

Serves: 6

1 pound venison, ground
1/2 cup chopped onion
1/4 cup sweet green pepper, diced
1 teaspoon garlic powder
1 teaspoon prepared yellow mustard

2 teaspoons cumin
3/4 cup ketchup
1 tablespoon dark brown sugar
dash pepper
6 sandwich buns

In skillet, brown venison and onion, drain fat. Combine remaining ingredients in small bowl. Add to pan and simmer until flavors are blended and sauce thickens. Spoon meat onto buns.

TAKE YOUR TIME

Give yourself plenty of time to process your deer. Carefully remove sinew and fat from the meat before wrapping it. Fat begins to break down once meat is frozen, and it can taint the meat. It is also wise to bone-out as much meat as possible. Bones not only take up valuable freezer space, they can cause an off-flavor in meat if left in the freezer for too long.

(Grd) *Sloppy Spiced Joes*

I like to use chunky-style salsa when preparing this dish to give it even more texture.

Serves: 6

1 pound venison, ground
1/2 cup chopped onion
1 teaspoon chili powder
1/2 teaspoon salt

1/2 (15-16 oz) jar of salsa
dash pepper
6 sandwich buns
6 slices of pepper jack cheese

In skillet, brown venison and onion. Drain fat, stir in remaining ingredients and simmer until flavors are blended and sauce thickens. Spoon onto buns and add cheese slices. Place under broiler, if needed, for a few seconds to melt the cheese.

(Grd) *Spaghetti Sauce with Venison*

The balance of flavors in this sauce make it a family favorite. In fact, it is the only way Dan will eat spaghetti.

Serves: 4-6 depending on sauce reduction

1 pound venison, ground, cooked
2 tablespoons olive oil
1/3 cup onion, finely chopped
1 large garlic clove, minced
1 tablespoon brown sugar
1/4 teaspoon dried oregano

1/4 teaspoon dried basil
1/2 teaspoon salt
1/2 cup water
1 teaspoon beef bouillon granules
1 28 oz can diced tomatoes

In 4-quart pot, heat the oil. Add the garlic and onion and sauté until soft. Add the basil, oregano, salt, sugar, water, bouillon and diced tomatoes. Cover and simmer 15 minutes. Remove the cover and add the cooked ground venison. Cook uncovered over medium-low heat 45 minutes, occasionally stirring until sauce thickens.

RICH SOURCE OF VITAMIN K
Venison contains high levels of Vitamin K1 and K2 because they are highly concentrated in a deer's bloodstream. Vitamin K is an anti-hemorrhagic agent and is a key component in the blood's ability to clot quickly. Scientists believe deer obtain these high levels of the vitamins by eating massive amounts of green, leafy vegetation in spring, summer and early fall.

Grd *Spanish Rice*

This recipe is quick to make and fills you up just as fast. I like to serve it with chips and salsa on the side.

Serves: 4

1 pound venison, ground
3/4 cup onion, chopped
2 cloves garlic, minced
1/2 cup green pepper, diced
1 15 oz can tomato sauce
1-1/2 cups water

1-1/2 cups quick cook rice,
  uncooked
1 tablespoon Worcestershire sauce
1/4 teaspoon salt
pepper

In skillet, brown venison, onion and garlic. Drain fat. Add green pepper and remaining ingredients. Cover and simmer over low heat until liquid is absorbed to desired consistency.

Grd *Zucchini Lasagna*

I use this recipe when the supply of zucchini from my garden is plentiful. I love the combined flavor of venison, tomato and zucchini.

Serves: 6

1 pound venison, ground
1 clove garlic, minced
1/4 cup onion, chopped
1 14 oz can diced tomatoes
1/4 teaspoon salt
1 teaspoon Italian seasoning
pepper

12 oz small curd cottage cheese
1 egg, beaten
1 tablespoon parsley flakes
1/4 cup dry bread crumbs
1 cup mozzarella cheese, shredded
6 cups zucchini sliced into
  1/4" rounds

Preheat oven to 350 degrees.
In skillet, brown venison, garlic and onion. Drain fat. Add diced tomatoes, salt, pepper and seasoning. In small bowl, blend cottage cheese, parsley and egg. Grease 8-inch square pan and place half of the zucchini in bottom. Sprinkle with bread crumbs. Spread in layers with half of cottage cheese, meat and tomato mixtures. Top with mozzarella. Repeat layers except mozzarella. Bake for 30 minutes.

NO NEED TO BLEED
  The time-honored task of "bleeding" a deer — cutting the dead animal's throat — has been proven to do nothing to further facilitate blood loss from the carcass. A more efficient practice of removing blood is to simply field dress the animal promptly, rinse the chest cavity with clean, cold water from a residential source, and then pat dry with toweling. Do not use lake or stream water, as both can contain potentially deadly bacteria.

(Grd) (RB) *Ring Bologna & Burger Sandwiches*

This is a great recipe to use up leftover ring bologna. Spring for the good, large hot dog buns—you'll fill them up.

Serves: 8-10

1 pound venison, ground
1/2 ring bologna, cut into 1/4" slices
1 teaspoon salt
dash pepper
2 teaspoons chili powder
1/4 teaspoon cumin
1 15 oz can tomato sauce

1/2 cup chopped onion
2 tablespoons green pepper, diced
2 tablespoons butter
1-1/2 tablespoons brown sugar
1-1/4 teaspoons balsamic vinegar
6 hot dog buns toasted

Preheat oven to 450 degrees.
In skillet, brown venison and drain fat. Add salt, pepper, chili powder, cumin and 1/2 can of tomato sauce. Simmer until blended. Spread mixture across buns covering entire exposed surface. Press ring bologna slices into buns. Bake at 450 degrees for eight minutes or until slightly browned and heated through.
In saucepan, cook green pepper and onion in butter. Add remaining tomato sauce, brown sugar and vinegar. Serve over warm sandwiches.

(RB) *Ring Bologna Noodle Bake*

Many times, I do the preparation work on the ring bologna and onions the night before, making this a quick fix after work.

Serves: 4

1 venison ring bologna, sliced into
1/4" thick medallions
1/4 cup onions, finely chopped
2 tablespoons butter
1 15 oz can condensed tomato
   sauce

1 teaspoon prepared yellow
   mustard
1 teaspoon brown sugar
2 cups rotini noodles, cooked
1/2 cup potato chips, crushed

Preheat oven to 350 degrees.
Brown ring bologna medallions and onion in butter until soft. Add sauce, mustard and brown sugar, then combine in 1-1/2-quart casserole with noodles. Put crushed potato chips on top. Bake in oven for 30 minutes.

ADD FAT WITH CARE
   The fact that venison is nearly void of fat is not always a good thing in the kitchen. In fact, some cuts, like roasts, chops and steaks, oftentimes need to have fat added (in the form of butter, olive oil or bacon grease) to keep them from drying out during the cooking process.

RB *Ring Bologna Pizza Pockets*

Great for deer camp and family movie nights, these pizza pockets are made in minutes.

Serves: 4

1 ring bologna, sliced into thin
   rounds
1 can pizza sauce

3/4 cup mozzarella cheese,
   shredded
2 tubes refrigerated pizza dough

Preheat oven to 425 degrees
Roll pizza dough into two large rectangles. Cut rectangles in half so you have four squares. Cut squares into quarters. Fill half of the triangles in the middle with sauce, ring bologna and cheese. Place remaining triangles on top and press seams together gently with a fork. Bake until tops start to brown.

Rst *Barbeque Sandwiches*

I like to prepare and serve this dish the first day of deer camp. Friends and guests can help themselves whenever they arrive, or snack later in the evening on the leftovers.

Serves: 20

3 pounds of venison roast
2 cups water
1/2 pkg onion soup mix
1 cup ketchup
1 cup hickory smoke-flavored
   barbeque sauce
2 tablespoons red wine vinegar

3 tablespoons brown sugar
2 tablespoons Worcestershire sauce
1-1/2 teaspoons chili powder
2 teaspoons garlic powder
1/2 teaspoon salt
sandwich rolls

Preheat oven to 350 degrees.
Place venison roast in roasting pan, cover with soup mix like a rub and add water to pan. Mix other ingredients except rolls, and add to pan, coating the roast. Cover and bake for 2-1/2 hours or to desired doneness, occasionally turning venison and adding additional water as needed. Shred venison with a fork and fill sandwich rolls.

PAPER, TWICE, NOT PLASTIC
When processing your own deer, be sure to double-wrap the cuts with quality freezer paper. Label each package, noting the contents and date processed. Two layers of freezer paper provide better insulation and keep the meat from getting freezer burn.

(Rst) *Italian Roast*

This basic roast incorporates traditional Italian flavors and is not sharp or bitter.

Serves: 6

3 pounds of venison roast	1 teaspoon beef bouillon granules
1 cup onion, sliced	1 tablespoon brown sugar
2 large garlic cloves, minced	1 15 oz can tomato sauce
1 teaspoon dried oregano	1/2 cup water

Preheat oven to 350 degrees.
Place venison in roasting pan and cook for 1-1/2 hours. Drain fat and add remaining ingredients, pouring over meat. Cover pan and bake an additional 1 1/2 to 2 hours until tender.

(Rst) *Italian Spicy Sandwiches*

A favorite during early bow season, I often substitute fresh, diced garden tomatoes and increase the water to 2/3 cup if needed.

Serves: 10

2 pounds of venison roast	1 teaspoon dried oregano
1 28 oz can diced tomatoes with juice	1 teaspoon garlic powder
1/3 cup water	2 teaspoons crushed red pepper
1/3 cup balsamic vinegar	1 teaspoon salt
1 teaspoon dried basil	sandwich rolls

Preheat oven to 350 degrees.
Place venison roast in roasting pan. Add tomatoes, water and vinegar. Mix remaining ingredients except rolls, add to pan, then cover. Bake for 2-1/2 to 3 hours, occasionally turning venison and adding additional water as needed. Shred venison with a fork and fill sandwich rolls.

ALLERGY ALERT
   If you suffer from allergies or eczema and have not handled a lot of deer, proceed with caution. A 1988 study published in the New York Times *reported* that less than one-half of 1 percent of all hunters are allergic to deer. Most allergy suffers report congestion, hives, asthma, sneezing, runny noses and swollen eyelids and lips when they come in contact with deer saliva, blood, hair and/or dander.

ⓡ *Roast with Beer*

This stove-top roast smells good and tastes even better. It takes a few hours to make, but it is worth the effort if you have time to spare.

Serves: 8

3 pounds of venison roast	2 tablespoons brown sugar
2 tablespoons vegetable oil	3-1/2 teaspoons red wine vinegar
1 cup water	1 teaspoon salt
1 beer	pepper
1 8 oz can tomato sauce	1/2 cup flour
1/2 cup onion, chopped	1/2 cup water

In Dutch oven, heat oil and brown roast. Add remaining ingredients and bring to a boil. Reduce heat and simmer, covered, 2-1/2 to 3 hours. Remove meat from pan, then remove fat from drippings and pour into saucepan. Blend 1/2 cup water with 1/4 cup flour and add to drippings. Cook and stir until gravy reaches desired thickness.

ⓢ *Balsamic Stir-Fry*

The vegetables in this stir-fry provide a variety of flavors and textures to accompany the venison.

Serves: 4

1 pound venison steak, sliced into 1/4" pieces	1/4 cup balsamic vinegar
	1 14 oz can diced tomatoes, drained
1 medium sweet red pepper, sliced	2 tablespoons olive oil
1 medium onion, sliced	prepared rice
1/2 cup zucchini, chopped	

Heat oil in skillet. Add venison steak slices and cook for three minutes. Remove fat. Add vegetables and balsamic vinegar and cook another couple of minutes until zucchini is crisp-tender and other vegetables are soft. Serve over rice.

TIPS FOR BEST BURGERS

The National Center for Home Food Preservation recommends storing ground venison in a freezer at 0 degrees Fahrenheit or colder for no more than five months. Ground-meat quality and flavor will deteriorate in the freezer over time. For best end results, thaw ground meat in the refrigerator or microwave, never at room temperature, before cooking.

Barbeque Steak Bake

I like to serve this kid-friendly dinner over rice. My children always ask for second helpings.

Serves: 6

2 large venison steaks, cut into 4 pieces	1/4 cup celery, minced
4 tablespoons flour	1 10-3/4 oz. can condensed tomato soup
salt & pepper to taste	2 tablespoons lemon juice
1/2 teaspoon garlic powder	2 tablespoons Worcestershire sauce
2 tablespoons vegetable oil	2-1/2 tablespoons brown sugar
1/4 cup onion, finely chopped	2 tablespoons prepared mustard

Coat steak with pepper, salt, garlic powder and flour. Brown in skillet in oil with celery and onion. Add other ingredients, stir and cover. Continue simmering for 1-1/2 hours or until tender.

Swiss Steak

I love the way this dish smells while it cooks. We serve this steak with buttered noodles and salad.

Serves: 4

1 pound venison steak, sliced thin	2 cloves garlic, minced
1/4 teaspoon salt	1 14 oz can diced tomatoes
dash pepper	1/2 cup mild salsa
2 tablespoons flour	1/4 cup beef broth
1 tablespoon vegetable oil	prepared buttered noodles
1 large onion, sliced	

Season meat with salt and pepper. Pound the flour into the meat, slice it, then brown it in a large skillet in oil. Place onion slices on top of meat, add remaining ingredients and cover. Simmer about 45 minutes until tender. Remove meat and reduce sauce until thickened. Pour sauce over meat and serve.

RECIPE FOR A CLEANER CARCASS

If intestinal contents spill into your deer's chest cavity, use special care in cleaning it up. Cold water will work, but even better is a 50/50 solution of water and white vinegar, according to researchers at the University of Wisconsin. Spraying the solution inside the carcass will help destroy bacteria.

The Best of The Rest

◈◇◈◇◈◇◈

Chapter 6:

Herbed, Seasoned & Spiced

 *Broccoli Bacon Casserole*

Broccoli Bacon Casserole is a comfort food staple in my house. The kids love anything with potato nuggets, and I love being able to get some broccoli in my kids.

Serves: 6-8

1 pound venison bacon, diced and cooked
1 package frozen potato nuggets
2 10-3/4 oz cans condensed cream of broccoli soup

1/2 pound broccoli
1 onion, diced
1-1/4 cups light sour cream
nonstick spray

Preheat oven to 350 degrees.
Wash and trim broccoli, then cook in boiling water 5 minutes. Drain and pat out as much water as possible with paper towels. Chop into bite-size pieces. In large bowl, combine condensed soup, broccoli, onion and light sour cream. Add potato nuggets and pour into greased 13-inch x 9-inch x 2-inch pan. Sprinkle bacon over the top, cover and bake for 45 minutes. Uncover and bake an additional 10 minutes until top is crisp.

NEW ZEALAND IS NO. 1
Raising captive deer for commercial venison purposes originated in New Zealand in the late 1950s. Farmers quickly learned that fallow and red deer were highly adaptable to large-scale farming operations. Today, New Zealand is home to more than 4,000 venison farms, which raise more than 1.8 million animals annually, which accounts for more than 50 percent of the world's commercial venison. According to the Deer & Elk Farmer Information Network, female red and fallow deer account for more than 75 percent of New Zealand's annual venison harvest.

Bratwurst Melt Open-Face Sandwich

These are always a game-day hit. If you love sauerkraut and brats, you will love these sandwiches — especially with a cold Wisconsin ale nearby.

Serves: 4

4 venison bratwurst, cooked	1 cup Swiss cheese, shredded
2 tablespoons butter	1 jar sauerkraut, drained
4 teaspoons flour	1 teaspoon prepared mustard
3/4 cup milk	4 slices pumpernickel bread

Preheat broiler.
In saucepan, melt butter and add flour to make a roux. Add milk and cook until thick and bubbly, whisk in cheese and mustard. Remove from heat and fold in sauerkraut. Cover and keep on low heat while preparing sandwiches. Cut sausages in half lengthwise and broil with the cut side down until heated through, about three minutes. Toast bread in toaster. Put heated brats on toast and cover with warm sauce.

 ## *German-Style Chops*

Tender meat and rich flavors — and a few friends to help finish off the stout — make for a great evening.

Serves: 4

4 venison chops	1/4 cup brown mustard
1 12 oz bottle of stout	3 cloves garlic, crushed
1/2 cup onion, sliced	

Caution: Use care to avoid flare ups and injuries when grilling with alcohol.
In quart-size bag, mix beer, onion, brown mustard and garlic cloves. Mix and reserve 1/4 cup of marinade for basting. Add meat and marinate overnight, occasionally turning bag over. Remove chops and grill, baste reserved marinade on chops during the last two minutes of grilling.

Grd *Apple Cranberry Relish Venison Burgers*

Fresh apple cranberry relish adds a bit of zip to these burgers. Splurge for the good burger buns!

Serves: 6

1-1/2 pounds venison, ground	**Apple Cranberry Relish (below)**
1 sweet onion, sliced	**6 bakery rolls**

In skillet, cook burgers to desired doneness. Toast buns and top with cooked burgers, sliced onion and relish.

Apple Cranberry Relish

2 Cortland apples, cored	**1 orange with peel on**
2 cups whole cranberries, quartered with seeds removed	**3/4 cup sugar**

Grind the apples, cranberries and orange in a food chopper. Add sugar and mix well. Keep chilled until ready to use.

Grd *Bacon Potato Burger*

These burgers are a meal in themselves. Make sure you have lots of napkins handy!

Makes: 12 burgers

2 pounds venison, ground, shaped into 12 patties to fit biscuits	**1 jar prepared beef or brown gravy**
2 cups prepared instant mashed potatoes, warm	**1 package of 12 large frozen biscuits, baked**
6 slices venison bacon, cooked and broken in half	**cheddar cheese, sliced**

Cook the venison burgers to desired doneness. Cut biscuit in half. Top one half of biscuit with burger patty, cheese, mashed potato, bacon strips and gravy, finishing with other half of biscuit on top.

WRAP IT UP

A trick to keeping venison roasts moist and succulent is to brown the roast quickly, then wrap it in aluminum foil before roasting it in the oven. The tightly sealed foil package will help keep the juices in the meat and provide a natural baste.

Company Corn Bread Salad

This dish has great flavors, colors and textures. Prep the meat, sweet peppers, onions, dressing, corn bread and bacon a day ahead of time and this goes together quickly to serve guests.

Serves: 10

1 pound venison, ground
1 package taco seasoning
3/4 cup water
1 package cornbread/muffin mix prepared in 8" square pan
1 cup light mayonnaise
1 cup light sour cream
1 package ranch salad dressing seasoning
2 15 oz cans black beans, rinsed and drained

2 15 oz cans whole kernel corn, drained
1 14 oz can diced tomatoes, drained
1 cup colored sweet peppers, chopped
1/2 cup chopped red onion
1 4 oz can chopped green chilies
8 bacon strips cooked until crispy and broken into bits
2 cups mild cheddar cheese, shredded

In skillet, brown venison and add taco seasoning and water, cooking to package specifications. Set aside. When cornbread is cooled, crumble half into 13-inch x 9-inch pan. In small bowl, mix mayonnaise, sour cream and ranch mix. Top corn bread in pan with half of the taco meat and one half of the following in order: ranch dressing, beans, corn, tomatoes, sweet peppers, onions, chili peppers, bacon bits and cheese. Repeat layering and serve warm.

Skillet Frittata

This frittata makes a great breakfast, brunch, breakfast or dinner entrée. Having children, I frequently receive requests for breakfast at dinner.

Serves: 4

1/2 pound venison, ground and cooked until brown
2 colored sweet peppers
1 small onion, chopped
2 cloves garlic, minced
1 tablespoon vegetable oil

6 eggs
1/2 cup milk
salt & pepper
2 tablespoons mild cheddar cheese, shredded

In skillet, sauté peppers, onion and garlic in olive oil until soft. In large bowl, whisk eggs, milk, salt and pepper. Pour into skillet with veggies. Sprinkle with meat and cheese. Cook like an omelet, lifting the edges to let the liquid go beneath until set. Cook about eight minutes.

(Grd) *Venison & Refried Bean Quesadillas*

The smoky taste of cumin adds great flavor to these quesadillas. They are game-day favorites at my house.

Serves: 4

1 pound venison, ground	1 cup Mexican cheese blend,
1/2 cup refried beans	shredded
1 4 oz can chopped green chilies	warm tortillas
1 teaspoon ground cumin	2 tablespoons melted butter
1/4 teaspoon salt	prepared guacamole

Preheat oven to 475 degrees.
In skillet, brown venison, drain fat. Add beans, green chilies, cumin and salt. Butter the tortillas on one side, then fill with meat and cheese. Bake for 10 minutes. Serve with guacamole.

(Grd) *Venison Burger Sandwiches*

I love a great Sunday afternoon sandwich that is easy to make. In fact, this one is always a favorite companion to a cup of soup or side salad.

Serves: 6

1 pound venison, ground	salt & pepper
1 small onion, diced	1 loaf French bread hollowed out
1 8 oz can tomato sauce	1 tablespoon melted butter
1/4 cup packed brown sugar	1 package American cheese slices
1 teaspoon garlic powder	

Preheat broiler.
In skillet, cook venison and onion until meat is cooked through. Drain fat. Add tomato sauce, brown sugar, garlic powder, salt and pepper. Bring to a boil, then simmer 10 minutes. Brush inside of bread loaf with melted butter. Put under broiler to toast, then remove from oven and fill with meat. Top with cheese slices and return to broiler until cheese is melted and slightly browned. Place top on the loaf and slice before serving.

THE HEART OF THE MATTER

Most folks who love venison liver will also find pickled venison heart a favorite for sandwiches and snacking. My brother-in-law never lets a whitetail heart go to waste. His key to preparing the heart is to trim it of all fat and sinew and then rinse it with cold water. Next, make six knife slits into the heart and pack with garlic cloves. Place it in a pot of equal amounts of water and cider vinegar (enough to cover) and boil for one hour. Cool, slice and serve.

(Grd) *Zucchini & Black Bean Quesadillas*

This recipe uses up extra zucchini from the garden during summer.

Serves: 6-8

1 pound venison, ground
1 package taco seasoning mix
3/4 cup water
3/4 cup shredded zucchini
1/4 cup shredded carrot
1 teaspoon ground cumin
1 teaspoon butter

1 15 oz can black beans, rinsed and
   drained
warm tortillas
1 cup Mexican cheese blend,
   shredded
3/4 cup salsa

In skillet, prepare ground venison with taco seasoning and water as directed. Remove from skillet. Add butter and cook zucchini and carrots with cumin until slightly softened, about two minutes, then add beans and cook for an additional two minutes. Remove from heat and stir in seasoned venison. Place mixture on tortilla and top with salsa and cheese. Fold tortilla in half and cook in skillet until cheese melts.

(RB) *Potato Pizza*

This pizza recipe does not include tomato sauce, and you won't miss it.

Serves: 4

1/2 ring bologna cut into bite-sized
   pieces
5 medium russet potatoes, peeled,
   boiled in water until cooked
   (about 25 minutes)
1 tube refrigerated pizza dough,
   baked at 350 degrees for 15
   minutes on a greased cookie sheet

1/4 cup milk
2 tablespoons vegetable oil
1 red onion, cut in half and sliced
1 colored sweet pepper, chopped
2 cups blended Monterey Jack and
   cheddar cheese, shredded

Preheat oven to 375 degrees.
Whip potatoes and milk using beaters. Spread over crust while still warm. In skillet, sauté vegetables in oil. Sprinkle over potatoes, then top with bacon and cheese. Bake for 20 minutes until cheese is lightly browned.

REMOVE NODES

Lymph nodes occur throughout a deer's body and act as filters for waste material. If you process your own deer, it is wise to learn the location of these nodes and remove them during the butchering process. Lymph nodes are gray or brown in appearance and appear as slippery ovals. They are located in major joints like those in the shoulder blades and hams.

🅡🅑 *Ring Bologna & Corn Scrambler*

All the great tastes of an omelet with the ease of scrambled eggs. Serve with toast and hash browns for a hearty opening day breakfast.

Serves: 4

2 cups ring bologna, diced
8 eggs, beaten
1/4 cup milk
1/4 teaspoon thyme

salt & pepper
2 packages frozen corn, thawed
1 cup mild cheddar cheese,
  shredded

In bowl, mix eggs, milk, thyme, salt and pepper. In large skillet, heat ring bologna and corn, then pour egg mixture over the top and scramble until cooked. Remove from stove, top with cheese and cover for a couple of minutes until cheese melts.

🅡🅑 *Ring Bologna & Peppers*

I love using fresh peppers from the garden to make this dish. It is a dish that I serve often in the summer, as it requires no oven.

Serves: 3

1/2 ring bologna cut into rounds
3 tablespoons vegetable oil
3 sweet colored peppers cut into
  wedges

1 cup water
1 cup onion soup mix
rice, prepared

In skillet, heat oil and brown ring bologna. Set aside on paper toweling. Sauté peppers to desired tenderness. Return ring bologna to skillet. Mix water and onion soup mix, then add to skillet. Cover and simmer for five minutes until thickened. Serve with prepared rice.

GROW YOUR OWN GARLIC

We love garlic with our venison, and that is why we plant it by the rows in our vegetable garden. It is easy to grow, but patience is required. Plant rows of single bulbs in fall for a crop next fall. Water frequently and weed between the rows to maximize production.

Garlic not only tastes good, it's good for you. For best antioxidant effects, age your garlic on racks in a cool, dry place (i.e.: basement or root cellar).

RB *Ring Bologna Mashed Potato Bake*

I love roasted garlic, mashed potatoes and venison ring bologna. This recipe combines them all in a great bake that you can keep warm in the oven for holidays and other special occasions.

Serves: 6-8

1/2 ring bologna, cut into large dice
1 garlic bulb, top cut off to expose
   cloves
olive oil
8 red potatoes, peeled and chunked
1/4 cup butter or spread
8 oz light sour cream

1/4 cup milk
1/4 small red onion, diced
salt & pepper
1 15 oz can whole kernel corn,
   drained
1 cup blended Monterey Jack and
   cheddar cheese, shredded

Preheat oven to 400 degrees.

Place garlic head in muffin tin cup. Drizzle with olive oil until coated, then cover heads with aluminum foil. Place in oven and roast for about 30-35 minutes until cloves are soft. Remove from oven and set aside. Reduce oven to 350 degrees. Place potatoes in small stockpot and cover with water. Bring to a boil and simmer for about 20-25 minutes. Drain. Squeeze cooled garlic into bowl. Add potatoes when cool enough to handle. Mix in remaining ingredients except corn, ring bologna and cheese with a mixer on medium speed. Stir in corn and ring bologna and pour into large greased casserole. Top with cheese and bake for 25 minutes or until heated through and the cheese is melted and lightly browned.

RB *Microwave Ring Bologna Quesadillas*

Serves: 3-4

1/2 ring bologna sliced like
pepperoni
6 small flour tortillas

2 cups Mexican cheese blend
shredded lettuce
salsa

On one half of each tortilla, place slices of ring bologna and cheese. Microwave at half power for 35-40 seconds so cheese melts. Top with lettuce and salsa and fold in half. Repeat for all tortillas.

Ⓡⓢⓣ *Garlic-Infused Venison Roast*

I love garlic, so this is one of my favorite recipes. Also, rosemary and thyme are my two favorite herbs to use with venison.

Serves: 6-8

3 pounds venison roast
1 garlic bulb, cloves peeled
2 teaspoons dried rosemary, crushed
1 teaspoon onion powder
1 teaspoon garlic powder
1/2 teaspoon dried thyme

1 cup baby carrots, halved
16 white pearl onions
1 tablespoon beef bouillon granules
3 tablespoons cornstarch
1/3 cup water

Cut slits in roast and press garlic cloves into them. In a small bowl, make a rub of the rosemary, onion powder, garlic powder and thyme. Coat the roast with the rub. Put roast into a quart-size plastic bag and refrigerate for several hours.
Preheat oven to 325 degrees.
Put roast and vegetables in roasting pan with water covering the bottom about 1/2-inch in depth. Sprinkle with granules and cook for 2-1/2 hours until roast is 160 degrees. Plate roast and vegetables. Mix cornstarch and water. Whisk into pan drippings and bring to boil. Continue to cook, whisking until gravy has thickened.

Ⓡⓢⓣ *Shredded Venison Roast*

Rosemary is one of my favorite herbs to use in venison recipes, and it's great in this shredded venison sandwich.

Serves: 8

3 pounds venison roast
2 cups water
1 tablespoon beef bouillon granules
1-1/2 teaspoons dried rosemary, crushed

1 teaspoon garlic powder
1 teaspoon onion powder
8 hamburger buns

Put venison in slow cooker. Add water. In small bowl, mix bouillon granules, rosemary, garlic powder and onion powder. Rub it onto the top of the roast. Cook on low for about six hours or until tender. Remove roast, shred and return to slow cooker. Serve venison on buns, using the extra gravy for dipping if desired.

ONCE A YEAR WON'T HURT YOU
Today's health experts shun the consumption of any organ meats, but, as they say, everything in moderation. This especially applies to the delicious meal of venison liver, which most hunters only eat once a year anyway. Besides, it is an excellent source of protein, iron, Vitamin A and Vitamin B.

Venison Egg Bake

Another simple and delicious breakfast or brunch dish bringing together the flavors of potato, cheese and venison.

Serves: 10

1 pound uncased, seasoned venison
  sausage cooked
8 large eggs
1/2 teaspoon dried rosemary,
  crushed
1 cup milk

pepper
2 10-3/4 oz cans condensed
  cream of potato soup
1 cup blended Monterey Jack and
  cheddar cheese, shredded
nonstick spray

Preheat oven to 375 degrees.
In bowl, whisk eggs, rosemary, milk and pepper, set aside. In skillet, pour soup over warm venison sausage. Pour egg mixture in and stir until blended. Pour in large casserole sprayed with nonstick spray, top with cheese and bake for 40-45 minutes until toothpick comes out clean.

Simple Sauced Steak

We love to grill our venison steaks. This sauce is easily made from staple ingredients in your spice rack.

Serves: 2

2 large venison steaks
3 tablespoons vegetable oil
1 teaspoon dried thyme
1 teaspoon dried garlic powder

1 teaspoon dried rosemary
1 teaspoon onion powder
1/4 teaspoon salt

In small mixing bowl, mix all ingredients except steaks. Cook steaks on grill to desired doneness. Baste sauce on steaks for the last two minutes of grilling time.

SPICE IT UP
If you like your venison chili with some kick, here's a tip: Embrace the chipotle chile pepper! Indigenous to Mexico and now a standard in horseradish-based sauces throughout the world, the smoked, ground pods of chipotle chiles can make a good pot of venison chili absolutely fantastic. You needn't use a lot to give your chili some zip. About one teaspoon of ground chipotle pods will provide plenty of spice for 8 cups worth of chili.

(Stk) *Steak Fajita Kabobs*

Quick to fix and full of flavor, these kabobs are great for backyard grilling.

Serves: 6

1 pound venison steak, sliced into
   1-inch strips
1/2 cup red wine vinegar salad
   dressing
1 teaspoon ground cumin
3 green sweet peppers, seeded with
   membranes removed and cut into
   chunks

1 red onion, wedged
sour cream
salsa
8-inch tortillas
metal or soaked wooden skewers

In quart-size plastic bag, combine salad dressing and cumin. Add venison and vegetables and marinate in refrigerator overnight. Remove steak and vegetables from bag and put on skewers. Grill to desired doneness. Wrap tortillas in foil and keep warm. Serve cooked kabobs with tortillas, salsa and sour cream.

(Stk) *Venison & Swiss Sandwich*

Red wine vinegar salad dressing makes a great marinade, especially when combined with sweet onions.

Serves: 6

2 pounds venison steak, sliced thin
1 sweet onion, sliced
3/4 cup red wine vinegar salad
dressing, divided

2 tablespoons horseradish mustard
6 slices of Swiss cheese
6 sandwich rolls

Placed sliced venison, onions and mustard and 1/2 cup salad dressing in a quart-size plastic bag and marinate for 24 hours, turning occasionally. Remove venison and onions from bag and put into skillet. Add remaining 1/4 cup dressing and cook to desired doneness. Serve on rolls with Swiss cheese.

THEY STARTED FROM SCRATCH
   Although New Zealand is the world's largest exporter of venison, deer are not native to the country. According to the Deer & Elk Farmer Information Network, New Zealand's first imported deer were brought from England and Scotland for sport hunting in the 1860s. The deer were released mainly in the lush Southern Alps and its foothills in the South Island.

Chapter 7:

Mushroom-Enhanced

(Bcn) *Mushroom, Bacon & Bean Casserole*

This is a great way to use your venison bacon in a side dish. This is a holiday favorite at our house.

Serves: 10-12

6-8 slices venison bacon diced &
  cooked
1 pound fresh mushrooms, sliced
1 onion, diced
2 tablespoons vegetable oil
1/4 cup flour
1 cup half 'n half

1 cup mild cheddar cheese,
  shredded
pepper
2 packages French-style beans,
  frozen, thawed and drained
1 can sliced water chestnuts, drained
roasted slivered almonds

In skillet, sauté mushrooms and onion in oil until they begin to soften, add flour to make a roux. Slowly add half 'n half and cook until thick and bubbly. Whisk in cheese and pepper and remove from heat. In 3-quart casserole, layer beans, water chestnuts, cheese sauce and almonds. Bake for 30 minutes.

(Brt) *Deer Camp Brat Bake*

This recipe is based on a school lunch I used to have growing up. It's good comfort food that's easy to bake.

Serves: 4-6

1 pound venison brats with casing
  removed
1 package frozen potato nuggets
1 onion, diced
1 can 10-3/4 oz condensed
  cream of broccoli soup

16 oz sour cream
1 teaspoon rosemary, crushed
2 cups mild cheddar cheese,
  shredded
nonstick spray

Preheat oven to 350 degrees.
Layer potato nuggets on bottom of sprayed 13-inch x 9-inch x 2-inch baking dish. In skillet, cook venison and onion until cooked through, then layer over nuggets. In bowl, mix soup, sour cream and rosemary, then spread over meat. Top with cheese and bake for 35 minutes until cheese melts and browns slightly.

(Grd) *Acorn Squash & Mushroom Bake*

I grow a ton of acorn squash in my garden every year. I cut them in half and place them on cookie sheets at 350 degrees until the shells are soft, about 45 minutes to an hour. I scoop out the pulp when they have cooled and freeze the pulp to have as a side vegetable or to use in recipes such as this one.

Serves: 4-6

1 pound venison, ground and cooked
2 cups whipped (with beater) acorn squash
1 10-1/2 oz can condensed cream of mushroom soup
1 4 oz can chunky Portabella mushrooms, drained

1 cup light sour cream
1 small onion, diced
salt & pepper
3 cups herb-seasoned stuffing, divided
2 tablespoons melted butter
nonstick spray

Preheat oven to 350 degrees.
In large bowl, stir the cooked venison, squash, mushroom soup, mushrooms, sour cream, onion, salt and pepper to taste. In 1-1/2-quart casserole coated with nonstick spray, cover bottom with 1-1/2 cups stuffing. Add mushroom mixture and top with remaining 1-1/2 cups stuffing with the melted butter drizzled over the top. Bake for 35 minutes until top is brown.

(Grd) *Classic Sesame Venison & Noodles*

A classic meal made with the ease of modern convenience is a true comfort food in my book…enjoy!

Serves: 4

1 pound venison, ground
1 10-1/2 oz can condensed French onion soup
1/2 cup prepared beef gravy
1 4 oz can chunky Portabella mushrooms, drained

1 tablespoon flour
1 tablespoon water
sesame seeds
prepared egg noodles

In skillet, brown venison and remove fat. In bowl, blend soup, gravy and mushrooms. Pour into skillet, boil and simmer covered for 5 minutes. In small bowl, blend flour and water until smooth. Stir into venison mixture, boil and stir until gravy thickens. Serve over noodles. Sprinkle top of dish with sesame seeds.

(Grd) *Spinach & Venison Stuffed Portobellos*

A word on the mushrooms: Both spellings of Portobello are commonly used. I have used Portabella where the brand I use refers to them as such, and Portobello where the brand I use refers to them as the latter. All I really need to know is they are delicious with venison and I hope you like them.

Serves: 4

1/4 pound venison, ground and
   cooked until brown
4 large Portobello mushrooms
2 tablespoons vegetable oil
1 14 oz can diced tomatoes, drained
1 package frozen chopped spinach,
   thawed with liquid squeezed out

1/4 cup scallions, sliced
1/2 teaspoon dried rosemary,
   crushed
1/2 cup mild cheddar cheese,
   shredded

Preheat oven to 375 degrees.
Scoop out mushroom stems and gills. Sauté in large skillet over medium heat until tender, about 10 minutes. Remove from skillet and place on baking sheet. In small bowl, combine all ingredients except cheese. Fill mushroom caps, top with cheese. Bake 10 minutes or until heated through.

(RB) *Ring Bologna Mashed Potato Casserole*

Potatoes, sour cream, mushrooms and venison in one easy meal without a lot of dishes, I don't think you can go wrong in that scenario.

Serves: 6

1 venison ring bologna, sliced
4 large russet potatoes, peeled and
   cut into 4-6 chunks
1/2 cup sour cream
1 teaspoon dried thyme
1/4 cup beef broth
1/2 pound fresh mushrooms, sliced

2 small garlic cloves, minced
1 large onion, chopped
1/4 cup mild cheddar cheese,
   shredded
1 teaspoon parsley
nonstick spray

Preheat oven to 350 degrees.
Boil potatoes in water until soft, about 20-25 minutes. Remove with slotted spoon and transfer to mixing bowl. Add sour cream, thyme and broth and use a mixer to beat them smooth. In skillet, cook ring bologna, mushrooms, garlic and onion until heated through tender. Put half the potato blend into the bottom of a casserole sprayed with nonstick spray. Top with meat mixture, cover with remaining potato mixture and top with cheese and parsley. Bake for 15 minutes or until cheese is melted and slightly brown.

(Rst) *Shredded Venison & Cheese Pizza*

If you are like me when it comes to eating cheese steak sandwiches, you'll love this classic sandwich as a pizza.

Serves: 3-4

1 cup cooked and shredded venison
   roast
2 teaspoons olive oil
2 small, colored sweet peppers
2 4 oz cans chunky Portabella
   mushrooms, drained
1 small white onion, sliced

3 cloves garlic, minced
1 Italian bread shell crust
Roma-style pizza sauce
2 oz cubed cream cheese
2 cups provolone cheese, shredded
1/2 teaspoon dried oregano

Preheat oven to 450 degrees.
Sauté sweet peppers, onion, mushrooms and garlic in oil. Place pizza shell in pizza pan, top with pizza sauce, dot with cream cheese, cover with pepper, onion, mushroom and garlic mix, shredded venison, oregano and provolone cheese. Bake for 10 minutes or until cheese is melted.

(Rst) *Coffee & Mushroom Roast*

One year, we didn't have beef broth at camp, but we did have a lot of strong coffee around. Here is the result.

Serves: 8

4 pounds venison roast
2 teaspoons vegetable oil
1 onion, sliced
2 4 oz cans chunky Portabella
   mushrooms, drained
3 cloves garlic, minced
1-1/2 cups potatoes, cubed

1 cup baby carrots, chopped
salt & pepper
1-1/2 cups strong brewed coffee
1 teaspoon chili powder
1/3 cup water
3 tablespoons cornstarch

In skillet, sauté onions and garlic until soft. Add mushrooms until heated through, remove from skillet and set aside. Place carrots and potatoes in large slow cooker. Salt and pepper the roast, then brown it in the same skillet. Place meat in slow cooker on top of vegetables, then top with mushroom mixture. Pour coffee over the top, then sprinkle with chili powder. Cook for six hours or until meat is tender. Remove roast and vegetables from cooker. In small bowl, combine water and cornstarch until smooth. Raise temperature in the cooker to high and cook about 15 minutes until gravy is thickened.

(Stk) *Granny Smith Stir-Fry*

This stir-fry combines venison-friendly apples, mushrooms and pecans.

Serves: 4

1 pound venison steak sliced into
thin strips
2/3 cup water
3 tablespoons apple juice
concentrate
3 tablespoons soy sauce
2 teaspoons cornstarch
1/2 teaspoon ground ginger

1 tablespoon olive oil
1 4 oz can chunky Portabella
mushrooms, drained
2 red sweet peppers sliced into
strips
1 Granny Smith apple, sliced thinly
1/4 cup pecans, chopped very fine
rice, prepared

In small bowl, combine water, concentrate, soy sauce, cornstarch and ginger. Heat oil in skillet over medium heat. Add mushrooms, peppers and apples, cooking until apples and peppers begin to soften. Add venison and cook until medium-rare. Add sauce and nuts to pan and cook until desired doneness is reached. Serve over prepared rice.

(Stk) *Mushroom-Topped Steaks*

Get the mashed potatoes ready for these steaks. They are a fast, simple and delicious meal!

Serves: 4

4 venison steaks
1 tablespoon Dijon mustard
1/2 cup red wine

2 tablespoons vegetable oil, divided
2 4 oz cans chunky Portabella
mushrooms, drained

In large skillet, heat 1 tablespoon oil. Put mustard in plastic bag and add steaks one at a time, coating them in the mustard. Cook steaks in skillet until medium and remove. Add 1 tablespoon oil to skillet with mushrooms and red wine. Simmer for about two minutes, then pour over steaks.

DEER OF THE WORLD

Sika deer — indigenous to China, Taiwan, Japan and Siberia — produce venison that is regarded by many as the most flavorful of all deer species. There were originally 13 subspecies of sika deer in mainland China, but today only three remain. The country's wild population is estimated to be less than 10,000 animals, but more than 275,000 are raised in captivity.

ⓢ *Mushroom Venison Stroganoff*

Any fancy looking dish with a simple preparation is considered a winner in my busy household. I hope that this will be a hit in your home.

Serves: 6

1 pound venison steak sliced into
  thin strips
2 tablespoons butter
1 4 oz can chunky Portabella
  mushrooms, drained
1 10-1/2 oz can condensed
  cream of mushroom soup

2 cups light sour cream
1 cup onion, chopped
1 teaspoon dried thyme
egg noodles, prepared

In skillet, brown steak in melted butter. Remove from heat and add mushrooms until heated through, return steak to skillet, add remaining ingredients except noodles. When heated through, serve over prepared noodles.

ⓢ *Venison Sausage & Mushroom Bake*

I love the fact that this dish bakes in the oven, which means less time for me standing over the stove in the morning, and more time for me to enjoy a cup of coffee.

Serves: 6

1 pound venison sausage, uncased
  and cooked
1/2 cup red onion, diced
1 4 oz can chunky Portabella
  mushrooms, drained
1 14 oz can diced tomatoes, drained
2 cups mild cheddar cheese,
  shredded

1 dozen eggs
3/4 cup milk
1 cup dry pancake mix
1/2 teaspoon thyme
salt & pepper

Preheat oven to 350 degrees.
In 3-quart casserole, mix first five ingredients. In large bowl, whisk eggs, milk, pancake mix, thyme, salt and pepper. Pour mixture into casserole. Bake for 45 minutes or until cooked through.

OF CHEESE & VENISON
  Of the 42 U.S. states with huntable whitetail populations, Wisconsin leads the way when it comes to venison generosity. In 2009, Wisconsin celebrated the 10th anniversary of its widely popular venison donation program. With the aid of Department of Natural Resources' funds, state hunters donated more than 3.1 million pounds of venison to food pantries over the previous decade. All tolled, hunters donated more than 70,000 deer to the program, which is a partnership between the DNR and local charitable organizations.

Chapter 8:

Soups & Stews

(Bcn) *Venison Bacon Corn Chowder*

This hearty chowder is a great way to use up some extra venison bacon.

Serves: 6

6 slices venison bacon, cooked and
   drained
1 tablespoon vegetable oil
1 onion chopped
2 15 oz cans whole kernel corn,
   drained

1 cup potatoes, cooked and diced
1 10-1/2 oz can condensed
   cream of mushroom soup
2-1/2 cups milk
salt & pepper to taste

Heat oil in skillet. Add onion and cook until soft, add remaining ingredients except bacon, bring to boil then simmer 5-10 minutes. Serve in bowls with bacon crumbled on top.

(Grd) *Mexican Venison Soup*

A quick way to use up some extra ground venison, the flavors and texture of this soup are great.

Serves: 6

1 pound venison, ground
1 small red onion, diced
1 10-1/4 oz can diced tomatoes
1 4 oz can chopped green chilies

1 12 oz can whole kernel corn,
   drained
4 cups Mexican blend cheese,
   shredded

In large saucepan, cook venison and onion until meat is cooked through, remove fat. Stir in remaining ingredients and continue cooking and stirring until cheese is melted.

VENISON'S PLACE IN WORLD HISTORY

According to research conducted by the New York *Times* in the early 1990s, venison's roots as a staple food can be traced back to wild sika populations that roamed China more than 500,000 years ago. The researchers also report that excavations in France indicate that venison was the third most important food source for inhabitants of that region 110,000 years ago. The top two? Horse and wild boar!

(Grd) *Vegetable Venison Stew*

I love the way this stew smells while it cooks. It goes great with a grilled cheese sandwich.

Serves: 6-8

1 pound venison, ground
1 14-1/2 oz can stewed tomatoes
with onions, celery & green peppers
1 cup baby carrots, chopped into
　thirds

2 russet potatoes, cubed
2 cups water
1/2 cup long grain rice
salt & pepper

In stockpot, cook venison until meat is cooked through. Remove fat, add the remaining ingredients and bring to a boil. Reduce heat and simmer 30 minutes, covered, then remove cover and simmer an additional 20 minutes or until desired thickness is reached.

(RB) *Harvest Moon Soup*

This soup provides another great way to use the acorn squash from the garden and the venison in the freezer.

Serves: 4-6

1 venison ring bologna, cut into
　large dice
16 pearl onions
3 cloves garlic, minced
4 cups water
1 cup baby carrots, chopped into
　thirds

3 russet potatoes, cubed
1 cup acorn squash peeled and
　chopped
1 tablespoon beef bouillon granules
1 teaspoon dried thyme
1 10-1/4 oz can diced tomatoes

In stockpot, add all ingredients except tomatoes and bring to a boil. Reduce heat and simmer, covered, for 20 minutes. Add tomatoes and cook covered until vegetables reach desired tenderness.

WHEN POACHING BROUGHT THE DEATH PENALTY
　Americans who complain about having to hunt deer on crowded public lands would be best served to learn more about the struggles of Europe's commoners. According to researchers at American University in Washington, D.C., Europe's Forest Law essentially outlawed deer hunting by commoners in about 800 A.D. The law, passed shortly after the fall of Rome, regulated the use of all woodlands to the deeded gentry. Although commoners were allowed to pursue small game, big-game animals were considered private property of the upper class. Violators were subject to corporal punishment.

(RB) *Potato, Broccoli & Corn Chowder*

I love the textures of this chowder, and it looks great.

Serves: 10-12

1 venison ring bologna, cut into
  large dice
3 tablespoons vegetable oil
1 red onion, diced
1/2 cup celery chopped
1/4 cup flour
4 cups milk

4 large russet potatoes, cubed
2 10-3/4 oz cans condensed
  cream of broccoli soup
salt & pepper
1 cup of baby carrots, sliced in half
1/2 package frozen beans, cut
1 10-3/4 oz can creamed corn

In large stockpot, soften red onion and celery in oil. Sprinkle with flour and make a roux. Slowly add the milk, whisking until thick. Add remaining ingredients except corn and simmer covered for 35-40 minutes until vegetables reach desired tenderness. Stir in creamed corn and heat through.

(Rst) (Stk) *Apple Juice Stew*

Easy to make and full of flavor, this stew smells great and fills you up on a chilly fall day. It makes enough to serve our deer camp.

Serves: 12

2 pounds venison, cubed
24 ounces frozen mixed vegetables,
  thawed and drained
1 4 oz can chunky Portabella
  mushrooms, drained
1/4 cup onion, diced
2 envelopes brown gravy mix

2 tablespoons onion soup mix
1/4 teaspoon cinnamon
1 10-1/2 oz can beef broth
1 8 oz can tomato sauce
1-1/3 cup apple juice
3 tablespoons cornstarch
1/4 cup cold water

In large slow cooker set on low, place vegetables, mushrooms and onions. In quart-size resealable plastic bag, add gravy mix, soup mix and cinnamon. Add venison in batches to bag, shaking to coat, then add to cooker. In small bowl, mix broth and tomato sauce and pour over top of meat. Cook for six hours or until tender. Combine cornstarch with water and pour into cooker. Turn temperature to high for 10-15 minutes until desired thickness is reached.

A VORACIOUS APPETITE FOR VENISON

The average gray (timber) wolf will kill and eat about 15 to 20 deer annually, according to research compiled by the International Wolf Center of Minnesota. With the average white-tailed deer yielding about 40 pounds of venison per carcass, the average adult wolf would consume between 600 to 800 pounds of venison per year. With an estimated population of 2,900 wolves, Minnesota loses between 40,000 to 60,000 deer annually to these hungry canines.

(Rst) (Stk) *Sweet Molasses Stew*

This stew is a great smelling slow cooker favorite at my house, especially around the winter holidays.

Serves: 6-8

2 pounds venison, cubed
1 tablespoon vegetable oil
1 cup baby carrots, chopped into
  thirds
2 russet potatoes, cubed
1 large onion, sliced

1 14 oz can diced tomatoes
3/4 teaspoon ground ginger
4 tablespoons tapioca
1/4 cup cider vinegar
1/4 cup molasses

In skillet, brown meat in oil. Put carrots, potatoes, onion, tomatoes and ginger in slow cooker. Sprinkle with tapioca. Add venison, vinegar and molasses, cover and cook on low for 9 hours or until tender.

(Sge) *Venison Sausage & Black Bean Soup*

This soup tastes great on a brisk fall evening. It fills the whole house with great smells, so expect company in the kitchen while you are cooking.

Serves: 4

1/2 pound venison sausage cooked
  and cut into bite-sized pieces (boil
  sausages in water for 20 minutes
  to cook)
1 10-1/2 oz can beef broth
1 cup water
1 cup onion, diced

10 cloves garlic, minced
1 teaspoon dried oregano
2 15 oz cans black beans, drained
  and rinsed
2 14 oz cans diced tomatoes
1/3 cup sour cream

In stockpot, add beef broth, water, onion, garlic, oregano, sausage and black beans. Bring to boil, then simmer covered for 15 minutes, add tomatoes and cook another five minutes until heated through. Serve with sour cream on top.

DISCARD THE BONE SAW

Some hunters prefer to use a hand saw, hair-wire saw or simple axe to break the deer's pelvic bone during the field-dressing process. Separating the pelvis allows for quicker cooling and, when done properly, easier removal of the offal, bladder and anus. The hunters in my family prefer not to use this method because it greatly increases the odds of contaminating the upper rounds of the hindquarters with the deer's fecal matter and/or urine. What's more, opening up the pelvis exposes more meat to oxidation, which, in turn, renders those portions unusable due to increased blood pooling and drying.

ⓢ *Creamy Steak Soup*

Rosemary , fresh mushrooms and venison are a natural match. I love to grow and dry my own herbs for cooking great meals such as this one.

Serves: 4

1 pound venison, cubed
2 tablespoons vegetable oil
1 cup fresh mushrooms, sliced
3 small cloves garlic, minced
1/4 cup onion, diced
1/4 cup butter

1 10-3/4 oz can condensed cream of
   mushroom soup
1 cup half 'n half
1/4 teaspoon dried rosemary,
   crushed

In skillet, cook cubed venison in oil. In large saucepan, sauté mushrooms, garlic and onion in butter. Stir in soup, half 'n half and rosemary. Heat until hot but not boiling.

ⓢ *Tender Cider Stew*

Venison and apple…I can't think of a more natural combination, especially as I sit here looking out the window at the apple trees in my parent' s backyard while the deer snack on the windfalls around them.

Serves: 6

1 pound venison, cubed
1 tablespoon vegetable oil
1 cup baby carrots, chopped into
   thirds
2 russet potatoes, cubed
1 large onion, sliced

2 Granny Smith apples, peeled,
   cored and cubed
2 tablespoons tapioca
1 cup apple cider
1 10-1/2 oz can beef broth

In skillet, brown venison in vegetable oil. In slow cooker, put carrots, potatoes, onions, apples and venison. Sprinkle in tapioca. In large measuring cup or small bowl combine cider and broth and pour into slow cooker. Cook covered on low for eight hours or until tender.

THE BEST BLADES FOR DEER PROCESSING

Deer blood contains high levels of sodium (salt), which can corrode a knife blade very quickly, resulting in a dull blade if you don't take care of your equipment. Perhaps that is why veteran hunters immediately wash their knives in clear, cold water immediately after field-dressing and skinning procedures. According to the knife experts at *Blade* Magazine, the best hunting knives are those made of chromium stainless-steel alloys that are heat-treated to a hardness level of 60 Rc.

Chapter 9:

Sweet & Savory

(Grd) *Sweet & Sour Venison Loaf*

I like to use cider vinegar in sweet and sour sauces, because it gives a little extra kick.

Serves: 8-10

2 pounds venison, ground
2 eggs
1 cup dry bread crumbs

2/3 cup chopped onion
1 tablespoon Worcestershire sauce
salt & pepper

In large bowl, add all meatloaf ingredients and 1/2 of the sauce (recipe follows) and mix just until blended. Do not overwork the meat or your loaves will be tough. Form loaves in two 8-inch x 4-inch x 2-inch loaf pans and top with remaining sauce. Bake for 50-60 minutes and let stand 10-15 minutes before slicing.

Sauce
2 cups water
5 tablespoons brown sugar
5 tablespoons cider vinegar
2 tablespoons cornstarch

2 tablespoons corn syrup
2 tablespoons soy sauce
1/2 teaspoon salt

In a large saucepan, combine sauce ingredients and bring to boil. Whisk until thickened then set aside.

(RB) *Sweet & Sour Slow Cooker Ring Bologna*

As you might have figured out by the number of recipes I have included, we like our venison ring bologna. Actually, we love all of our venison, but our kids seem to like ring bologna the best.

Serves: 4-6

1 venison ring bologna, cut into
  rounds
1 can pineapple chunks with juice
1 cup baby carrots, halved lengthwise
1 colored sweet pepper, cut into
  chunks
1 red onion cut in half and then sliced

1/3 cup dark brown sugar, packed
2 tablespoons soy sauce
1/2 teaspoon garlic powder
1/2 teaspoon ground ginger
2 tablespoons cornstarch
1/4 cup water
prepared rice

Put all ingredients except cornstarch, water and rice in slow cooker. Cook on low for four hours. In small bowl, whisk cornstarch and water. Turn cooker to high and add cornstarch and water mixture. Cook about 15 minutes until gravy is thickened. Serve over prepared rice.

(RB) *Sweet Apple Ring Bologna*

These ring bologna rounds are great in a tortilla wrap with lettuce. Their sweetness makes them a kid favorite. I also like to cook chops in apple juice to give them more depth of flavor.

Serves: 4

1 venison ring bologna, sliced into
   rounds
1/3 cup sweet apple juice

1/3 cup apple jelly
3 tablespoons maple syrup

In skillet, simmer ring bologna and apple juice covered for eight minutes. Drain out juice and add syrup and jelly, stirring to coat ring bologna in melted jelly.

(Stk) *Nutty Orange Stir-Fry*

When I was a teenager, one of my favorite meals to cook was orange chicken. I first ate it at a local Chinese restaurant and then learned to prepare it myself at home. I used to serve it with rice and salad. This recipe blends a taste of my past with the grownup tastes of today.

Serves: 4

1 pound venison, cut into bite-sized
   chunks
2 carrots, sliced or buy a small bag
   of the precut
2 tablespoons vegetable oil
3/4 cup orange juice

1/2 teaspoon ground ginger
1/3 cup honey
1/4 cup soy sauce
2 tablespoons cornstarch
1/2 cup whole cashews
prepared rice

In skillet, stir-fry carrots in oil for four minutes, then add venison and cook until desired doneness is reached. Set aside. In saucepan, whisk orange juice, ginger, honey, soy sauce and cornstarch. Whisk to a boil over medium heat, whisking until thick. Pour into skillet with venison and heat until meat is warm. Stir in cashews. Serve over prepared rice.

REMOVE THE ESOPHAGUS AND WINDPIPE?
Meticulous field-dressing work calls for the complete removal of the windpipe and esophagus. This work is best left to experienced hunters who know how to handle a knife. If you desire to remove these organs, grip the base of the esophagus where it meets the stomach. Hold it taut and carefully reach up and sever the windpipe as close to the throat as possible. In the final analysis, removing the windpipe (a hollow tube made of cartilage) is not really necessary when the weather is cold and the deer will not be hung for more than a few days.

(Stk) *Venison Fajitas*

These fajitas are pretty on your plate and taste great. They disappear fast, so make sure to get to the table on time!

Serves: 4

1 pound venison steak, sliced into
   thin strips
1/4 cup soy sauce
2 tablespoons brown sugar
2 tablespoons pineapple juice
1 tablespoon cornstarch

3 cloves garlic, minced
1/4 cup onion, diced
2 cups sweet red peppers, cut into
   strips
4 tortillas, warmed

In small bowl, mix soy sauce, brown sugar, pineapple juice and cornstarch. Heat oil in skillet then add peppers, garlic and onion. Once vegetables are softened, add venison and cook until medium-rare. Add sauce and cook until desired doneness is reached. Serve in warm tortillas.

BIRD WATCHERS: DON'T THROW OUT THE FAT!
Processing your own venison can be a satisfying experience for the whole family. You know where your meat is coming from, and you can trim the meat to your own specifications. When trimming the fat from your next deer, consider saving the tallow from the shoulders, spine and hind quarters of the deer. This thick, waxy layer ("tallow") makes for an ideal supply of suet for bird feeders. Downy woodpeckers, nuthatches and red-bellied woodpeckers quickly flock to tallow suet feeders. To save the tallow for winter bird feeding, simply store it in plastic bags in your freezer.

Chapter 10:

Tomato-Based

Grd *Bacon-Rolled Meatloaves*

The bacon and cheese add moisture to this classic meatloaf recipe. They also add flavor and make for a fancier presentation.

Serves: 8

2 pounds venison, ground	1/2 teaspoon salt
2 eggs, beaten	pepper
1/4 cup ketchup	12 bacon strips, regular not thick
1/3 cup onion, diced	
1 cup mild cheddar cheese, shredded	

Preheat oven to 375 degrees.
In large bowl, combine all ingredients except venison and bacon. Add venison, mixing just until blended. Do not over mix or you will have tough loaves. On waxed paper, line up six bacon strips horizontally. Form two loaves of the meat mixture the same width as the bacon strips you have laid out. Place one loaf on top of the bacon and roll up the loaf, remove the wax paper and secure the ends of the bacon with toothpicks. Repeat. Place on four-sided baking sheet or 13-inch x 9-inch x 2-inch baking pan. Bake for 50 minutes or until done.

Grd *Barbeque Baked Burgers*

I love cooking venison burgers in the oven because they are less likely to fall apart. Use whatever flavor sauce you like and serve with baked beans on the side.

Serves: 4

1 pound venison, ground	4 burger buns
1/4 cup barbeque sauce	lettuce
1/3 cup bread crumbs	cheese
1/4 teaspoon ground cumin	onion

Preheat oven to 350 degrees.
In large bowl, mix barbeque sauce and venison, then shape into four patties. In small bowl, mix bread crumbs and cumin. Dip burgers into breading and place on four-sided baking sheet. Bake for 10 minutes, turn and bake for additional 10 minutes or until cooked through. Put cheese on burgers when done and cover for five minutes until cheese melts. Serve on buns with toppings.

(Grd) *Burrito Bonanza*

These burritos are a great after-work meal. You can slice the scallions the night before and even cook the burger ahead of time.

Serves: 4-6

1 pound venison, ground	2 cups long grain rice, prepared
1 4 oz can chopped green chilies	1 jar salsa, divided
1/3 cup sliced scallions	10 small tortillas
1 can black beans, drained and	1 cup Mexican cheese blend,
rinsed	shredded, divided

Preheat oven to 350 degrees.
Spray 13-inch x 9-inch casserole with nonstick spray.
Brown venison in skillet, drain fat. Add chilies and scallions and heat through. Add beans, rice and 1 cup of salsa. Spoon meat mixture into middle of tortillas and top with cheese blend, roll and place seam side down in greased casserole. Cover with remaining salsa. Cover and bake for 30 minutes, remove from oven, sprinkle with cheese and return uncovered to oven to bake an additional five minutes until cheese melts and begins to brown.

(Grd) *Cabbage Joes*

Cabbage Joes are a grown-up twist on a kid favorite. We grow a mix of mini cabbages in our garden every summer. This is a great way to use them up, in addition to slaw and sweet and sour cooked cabbage.

Serves: 6-8

1 pound venison, ground	1/4 cup brown sugar
1-1/4 cup red cabbage, shredded	2 tablespoons lemon juice
1 onion, diced	1 tablespoon cider vinegar
3 tablespoons green pepper, diced	1 tablespoon prepared mustard
1 cup ketchup	8 burger buns

Brown venison in skillet and remove fat. Add vegetables, cooking until crisp-tender. In bowl, mix ketchup, brown sugar, lemon juice, vinegar and mustard. Add sauce to skillet, cover and simmer for eight to ten minutes until cabbage is desired tenderness. Serve on buns.

REAL REASONS FOR MARINATING
   The true art of marinating meat for the grill is not to add flavor to the meat. Marinating's real purpose is to break down an otherwise tough piece of meat, making it tastier through tenderness. Venison steaks typically require only six to eight hours of marinating time. Roasts are best left to marinate a full 24 hours before cooking. Injection marinades, although popular, are not necessary. To expedite the process, use a fork or thin, sharp knife to poke holes in the meat to allow the marinade to penetrate the meat and do its job.

(Grd) *Eggplant & Venison Casserole*

We use fresh eggplant from the garden to make this dish. I love the hint of cinnamon. This tasty dish could also be prepared with zucchini using Parmesan cheese.

Serves: 6

1-1/2 pounds venison, ground
1 medium onion, diced
1 14 oz can diced tomatoes, drained
2 pounds eggplant, cut into
  1/2" rounds
2 teaspoons oregano
1 teaspoon cinnamon

salt & pepper
3 tablespoons vegetable oil
1/4 cup flour
2 cups milk
2 eggs, slightly beaten
1/2 cup mild cheddar cheese,
  shredded

Preheat oven to 375 degrees.
In skillet, brown venison with onion. Add eggplant, onion, tomatoes, oregano, cinnamon and salt and pepper, simmering for 10 minutes. In saucepan, make a roux by mixing the oil and flour over medium heat. Add milk and cook until thick and bubbly, whisking occasionally. Remove from heat and whisk in eggs and cheese.
Bake for 30 minutes.

(Grd) *Enchilada Bake*

A casserole that will bust your buttons before it breaks your wallet, this recipe is great to serve at parties.

Serves: 8

1 pound venison, ground
3/4 cup scallions, chopped
3 small cloves garlic, minced
1/3 cup flour
1-2 tablespoons chili powder
4 cups water

nonstick spray
12 warm tortillas
1 jar salsa
1 cup cheddar cheese, shredded
  and divided
sour cream

In skillet, brown meat with scallions and garlic, drain fat, sprinkle flour and chili powder over the meat, add water and boil. Reduce to simmering and cook covered for seven to eight minutes. Spray bottom of casserole with nonstick spray then line with 6 tortillas. Layer with venison mixture then 1/3 cup cheese and repeat process with remaining tortillas, 1/3 cheese, and salsa on top. Bake for 20 minutes, then place final 1/3 cup of cheese on top and cook until cheese is melted and lightly browned. Serve with sour cream.

Grd *Chili Corn Bread Oven Bake*

This recipe is great as the biscuits bake right in the chili, infusing them with great flavor.

Serves: 6

1 pound venison, ground
1 red onion, diced
1 15 oz can black beans, rinsed and
   drained
1 can whole kernel corn, drained
1 14 oz can diced tomatoes
1 4 oz can chopped green chilies
1 tablespoon chili powder

2 teaspoons ground cumin
1 teaspoon garlic powder
1 cup milk
1 cup cornmeal
1 cup flour
2 teaspoons baking powder
1/4 teaspoon salt
1 egg

Preheat oven to 400 degrees.
In roasting pan, brown venison and onion, remove fat. Add beans, corn, tomatoes, chilies, chili powder, cumin and garlic powder. Boil and reduce to simmer with cover on for 10 minutes to soften the mixture. In small bowl, mix cornmeal and milk and let sit for five minutes. Mix in flour, baking powder, salt and egg. Drop by spoonfuls onto chili and bake uncovered for about 15 minutes until biscuits are cooked through.

Grd *Mexican Pizza*

Taking only minutes to make, this affordable fresh-tasting pizza is a hit on a busy weeknight.

Serves: 4

1/2 pound venison, ground
1 package taco seasoning mix
3/4 cup water
1 Italian bread shell crust
1 jar salsa

1/4 cup scallions, sliced
2/3 cup Mexican cheese blend,
   shredded
2 Roma tomatoes, sliced
sour cream

Preheat oven to 425 degrees.
Prepare venison with taco seasoning with water as directed. Place bread shell on pizza pan. Spread with salsa and bake for five minutes. Sprinkle scallions, venison and cheese on top and cook an additional five minutes. Remove from oven and add sliced tomato and sour cream once it has cooled enough not to melt the sour cream.

(Grd) *Mini Cheddar Meatloaves*

My kids love when I make them these little loaves. I usually serve them with mashed potatoes and green beans.

Serves: 6-8

1 pound venison, ground
3/4 cup milk
1/2 cup quick-cook oats
1 cup mild cheddar cheese,
   shredded
1 small onion, diced

salt & pepper
8 oz tomato sauce
1/4 cup brown sugar, packed
1/2 teaspoon oregano
2 teaspoons prepared yellow
   mustard

Preheat oven to 350 degrees.
In mixing bowl, add milk and oats. Let stand for five minutes. Add egg, cheese, onion, venison, salt and pepper. In small bowl, stir tomato sauce, brown sugar, oregano and mustard. Coat the loaves with the sauce and bake 45 minutes or until desired doneness is reached.

(Grd) *Mini Meatloaf Cakes*

These are a fun dish for the kids to help out with. They are also a great part of a grab-and-go meal.

Serves: 6-8

1 pound venison, ground
1 egg, slightly beaten
1/2 cup prepared pizza sauce
1/4 teaspoon dried oregano
1/4 teaspoon dried basil

1/3 cup bread crumbs
4 slices of string cheese, cut into
   thirds
nonstick spray

Preheat oven to 375 degrees.
In mixing bowl, blend egg, sauce, herbs and bread crumbs, then mix in meat. Be careful not to over mix or meatloaf will become tough. In sprayed 12 cup muffin pan, push meat into bottom and sides. Push string cheese into middle of cakes. Bake for 18-20 minutes or until cooked through with cheese melted.

VENISON CONSUMPTION TRENDS UPWARD

It might sound trendy to "go green," but deer hunters and venison lovers worldwide seem to be taking it to a whole new level. While total consumption of food and beverages in North America and Western Europe is stagnating or merely reflecting population growth, organic food sales are growing at 20 percent annually, reports Russell Sawchuk of the Alberta Department of Agriculture, Food and Rural Development.

(Grd) *Quick Venison & Beans*

I like to make this after work. I love using the sweet maple-flavored beans, but feel free to use something with a little more punch to suit your tastes.

Serves: 4

1 pound venison, ground
1 clove garlic, minced
1 onion, chopped
1 can 28 oz maple baked beans

1/4 cup barbeque sauce
1 cup mild cheddar cheese,
  shredded

In skillet, cook venison, onion and garlic until venison is browned, remove fat. Stir in sauce and beans cooking over medium heat until heated through. Top with cheese and serve when melted.

(Grd) *Ranch Hand's Chili*

Warning: Don't use cheap beer in this recipe! Its flavors are worth the cost of a good bottle.

Serves: 6

2 pounds venison, ground
4 cloves garlic, minced
1-1/2 cups onion, diced
3/4 cup sweet green pepper, diced
2 tablespoons cornmeal
2 tablespoons chili powder
1 teaspoon ground cumin

1 14 oz can diced tomatoes
1 4 oz can chopped green chilies
1 15 oz can black beans, drained
  and rinsed
1 bottle quality beer
2 teaspoons salt
pepper to taste

Brown venison in large stockpot with garlic, onions and green peppers. Add cornmeal, chili powder, cumin, tomatoes, chilies, beans, beer, salt and pepper. Cover and simmer 90 minutes until thickened.

SAVE MONEY ON YOUR MARINADE

Many old-time deer hunters use plain cola to improve the tenderness of neck roasts, round steaks and rump roasts. Simply place the cut of meat in a 2-gallon plastic zip-shut bag. Add one can of cola, 1 cup of vegetable oil and seasonings to taste (four cloves of garlic, salt, pepper, etc.). Close the bag and place meat-soaked mixture in a large glass bowl and place in the refrigerator for 24 hours. Turn bag throughout the course of the day to help the marinade penetrate the meat. The acid from the cola will help break down the meat fibers and allow the seasonings to soak into the tissues.

Grd *Salsa Pizza*

These pizza slices make a great party appetizer or a great meal.

Serves: 6-8

1 pound venison , ground
1 package taco seasoning mix
3/4 cup water
2 tubes refrigerated pizza dough
1 jar salsa

2 cups Mexican cheese blend
1 can sliced black olives
shredded lettuce
light sour cream

Preheat oven to 400 degrees.
Prepare taco meat with venison, seasoning packet and water as directed.
Press pizza dough into cookie sheet. Spread with salsa, top with venison,
cheese and black olives. Bake for 15 minutes until crust is brown and cheese
is melted. Remove from oven and when slightly cooled, top with sour cream
and shredded lettuce.

Grd *Stuffed Tomato Cups*

*These are great for outdoor grilling. I usually grow early tomato varieties to make
these. Make sure to use a non-beefsteak variety.*

Serves: 6

1/2 pound venison, ground, cooked
1 pound fresh green beans, washed
  with tips removed cooked
1 15 oz can black beans, drained and
  rinsed
1 sweet red pepper sliced into strips
4 scallions, sliced
1/4 olive oil

1/4 cup red wine vinegar
1 teaspoon ground cumin
2 cloves garlic, minced
4 tablespoons fresh parsley, minced
salt & pepper
6 tomatoes with tops removed, pulp
  removed and juices drained out
  onto paper towels

In small bowl, whisk oil, half 'n half, vinegar, cumin, garlic and parsley. In large
bowl mix green beans, black beans, sweet peppers, scallions, salt, pepper
and parsley. Pour marinade over bean mixture and refrigerate for at least 30
minutes. Warm venison in skillet, then add bean mixture to skillet with slotted
spoon and heat until warm. Spoon into prepared tomato cups.

SAVE MEAT WITH CITRIC ACID
   When time is of the essence — and daytime temperatures are high — you can
drastically slow down the bacterial growth process by using food-grade citric acid.
Start by rinsing the inside of the deer carcass with cold water and patting dry with
paper toweling. Next, mix 2 ounces of citric acid powder with a quarter of water
and spray liberally on the inside of your field-dressed deer. The citric acid will slow
bacteria growth and deter flies from laying eggs on the exposed meat.

Grd *Taco Appetizer Pizza*

Easy appetizers are always a plus when entertaining. I cook the venison taco meat the day before so I can just heat it in the microwave while I make the rest of the pizza.

Serves: 8

1 pound venison, ground	1 14 oz can diced tomatoes, drained
1 8 oz tube refrigerated crescent rolls	2 scallions, sliced
1 package taco seasoning	1/4 cup sliced black olives
3/4 cups water	1/2 teaspoon ground cumin
sour cream	1-1/2 cups mild cheddar cheese, shredded

Preheat oven to 350 degrees.

Unroll crescent dough onto pizza plate and press to fit. Bake for eight to 10 minutes until lightly browned. Brown venison in skillet, then add taco seasoning and water, cooking to package specifications. Remove crust from oven and cool. Top with sour cream, taco meat, tomatoes, scallions and olives, dust with cumin and sprinkle cheddar cheese to cover. Cut into small squares to serve.

Grd *Taco Chip 'N' Dip*

This is a great way to let people serve themselves. I usually put out a few spoons with the dip. In addition to the chips, you will also need some napkins handy.

Serves: 10-12

1 pound venison, ground	1 14 oz can diced tomatoes, drained
1 package taco seasoning	1 4 oz can chopped green chilies
3/4 cups water	1-1/2 cups mild cheddar cheese, shredded
16 oz sour cream	
1/4 cup sliced black olives	scoop-shaped corn chips

Brown venison in skillet, then add taco seasoning and water, cooking to package specifications. Set aside to cool enough not to melt sour cream. In a 13-inch x 9-inch pan, spread sour cream, prepared taco meat, olives, tomatoes, chilies and cheddar cheese. Set out with chips.

THEY LOOK NASTY, BUT THEY ARE HARMLESS

Increased deer densities across North America have led to an increase in reported cases of papillomas, fibromas and papillofibromas on the carcasses of hunter-killed deer. These growths, which resemble large, fleshy black warts, are often found on the outer skin of a white-tailed deer. Although unsightly, the nodules are harmless and come off with the hide during the skinning process.

Taco Tartlets

These appetizers look great and taste even better.

Serves: 24+

1 pound venison, ground
1 package taco seasoning mix
3/4 cup water
2 loaves white bread, thinly sliced
3 tablespoons butter, melted

1/4 cup scallions, sliced
1 14 oz can diced tomatoes, drained
1 can sliced black olives
1 jar salsa
sour cream

Preheat oven to 350 degrees.
Prepare venison, taco seasoning and water as directed. Brush mini muffin cups with melted butter. Roll out bread with rolling pin to flatten and cut into 2-3/4-inch squares. Press into cups and bake for eight minutes or until toasted brown. Remove cups from oven, add venison and top with scallions, diced tomatoes, black olives, salsa and sour cream.

Tostada Mini Bites

This is another fun kid dish that could be used as an appetizer if desired.

Serves: 8

1 pound venison, ground
1 bottle mild picante sauce, divided
1 tube of 8 oversized refrigerated
 biscuits
1-1/2 cups lettuce, shredded

2 cups Mexican blend cheese,
 shredded
1 can sliced black olives
light sour cream

Preheat oven to 350 degrees.
Brown ground venison in skillet and remove fat. Add half of picante sauce to meat and stir until heated. Cut biscuits in half and roll out to rounds on cookie sheets. Bake for 10 minutes until brown. Top with venison, lettuce, cheese, black olives, sour cream and teaspoon of picante sauce.

TO SPLIT OR NOT TO SPLIT?
Deer hunters have developed several ways to field-dress a deer that will allow the carcass to cool quickly and efficiently. A common method used by many hunters is to slit open the stomach cavity, continuing all the way through the chest cavity and ending at the sternum. From there, some hunters use a stout blade or bone saw to split the chest cavity clear through to the base of the neck. We recommend against this practice, as it exposes more meat to oxidation and increases the chances of cross-contaminating the finished product with hair, dirt and other debris.

(Grd) *Venison & Corn-Stuffed Peppers*

This traditional meal is enhanced by pairing venison and corn in the stuffing.

Serves: 4

1 pound venison, ground
4 sweet green peppers
1/4 cup onion, diced
1 15 oz can whole kernel corn,
   drained

1 8 oz can tomato sauce
1/2 teaspoon Worcestershire sauce
1 10-1/2 oz can beef broth
1 cup cheddar cheese, shredded

Cut peppers in half removing seeds and membranes. Blanch for five minutes in boiling water. In skillet, brown venison and onion. Add corn, tomato sauce and Worcestershire sauce. Cook until heated through, about five minutes.
Fill peppers with stuffing and place in shallow baking pan. Add broth and cover with foil. Bake for 25 minutes, then uncover, sprinkle cheese on top and bake for an additional 15 minutes.

(RB) *Ring Bologna Ranch Pizza*

A great way to enjoy your ring bologna is on a pizza. The ranch dressing goes great with the venison, cheese and tomato flavors in this pizza.

Serves: 4-6

1/2 ring bologna sliced like
   pepperoni
1 Italian bread shell crust
1/2 cup tomato sauce

1/2 cup Italian cheese blend,
   shredded
1 small red onion cut in half
   and sliced
1/2 cup ranch dressing

Preheat oven to 450 degrees.
Place bread shell in pizza pan. Spread with tomato sauce, ring bologna and onion. Drizzle ranch dressing over the top and finish with cheese. Bake for 10 minutes.

CHOCK-FULL OF VITAMINS
   The vitamins and properties found in deer blood can assist with a wide range of human health conditions, according to Health Research Lab, a high-quality distributor of nutritional supplements. Scientists are still studying the exact properties in deer blood, but it is believed that high amounts of Vitamin A make it somewhat of a miracle supplement. For decades, Asian doctors have prescribed pills made from crushed antler velvet to treat diabetes, asthma, anemia, arteriosclerosis and stress-related problems.

Friends & Family

ⓡ *Charlie & Carla Alsheimer's Corned Venison*

3-5 pounds venison

2 quarts water

1/2 cup canning salt

1/2 cup quick curing salt product

2 tablespoons sugar

2 tablespoons pickling spice

4 bay leaves

8-10 whole black peppercorns

1-2 fresh garlic cloves, minced

Mix the brine ingredients in a large pot and bring to a boil. Let it cool completely.

Place 3-5 pounds of venison in a glass, plastic or ceramic bowl. (Do not use metal.) The cuts of meat should be no thicker than 2 inches with fat and silvery tissue removed. Pour the cooled brine over the meat and cover tightly with plastic wrap.

Refrigerate it for four to five days. At least once a day, turn the meat to circulate the brine.

Remove the meat from the brine and rinse it in cold water. Discard the brine. At this point, it is ready to be cooked in whatever way you would normally cook the particular cuts of meat that you use (oven, Dutch oven on the stovetop, pressure cooker, slow cooker, etc.) I prefer to can it in a pressure canner. Quarts require 90 minutes, pints take 75 minutes at 10 pounds pressure.

The corned venison works well in any corned beef recipe. We use it in Reuben sandwiches, barbecue and in a boiled dinner with cabbage, potatoes, carrots and onions.

ESTIMATE THE LIVE WEIGHT OF YOUR DEER

After studying the topic for months and conducting interviews with butchers and biologists across North America, *Deer & Deer Hunting Magazine* Editor Daniel E. Schmidt devised a formula for calculating the live weights of field-dressed deer. According to Schmidt, any hunter can obtain a ballpark estimate of his deer's live weight by multiplying the deers field-dressed weight by 1.28. For example, a yearling buck with a field-dressed weight of 112 pounds will have an estimated live weight of 143 pounds.

ⓡ *Charlie & Carla Alsheimer's Venison Stroganoff*

1 quart canned venison
2 large onions, sliced
1 beef bouillon cube
1 4 oz can mushrooms, drained
1 tablespoon Worcestershire sauce
1 tablespoon ketchup

1/4 teaspoon pepper
4-1/2 teaspoons cornstarch
1/2 cup sour cream
1-2 tablespoons prepared
horseradish
hot cooked noodles

Place onions in a large pan with the broth from the meat and the bouillon cube. Add water if necessary to make 1-1/2 to 2 cups of liquid. Cook for about 15 minutes, then add the mushrooms and meat. Continue to cook on medium heat until onions are tender. In a small bowl, combine the sour cream, cornstarch, Worcestershire sauce, ketchup, pepper and horseradish. Mix well. Gradually stir it into the venison mixture and cook five to 10 minutes longer until sauce is thickened. Serve over hot noodles.

ⓡ *R.G. Bernier's Canned Venison with Noodles*

Canned venison can be used in any recipe that calls for stew meat such as beef stew, meat pies, etc. Canned venison can be prepared quickly in any recipe, as it is already fully cooked, and has become a Bernier family favorite.

To prepare canned venison:
• You will need a pressure canner
• Take freshly cut venison and put in quart-size canning jars
• Put 1 teaspoon salt on top of meat in jar
• Process meat according to canner instructions

To prepare canned venison with noodles:
• Heat canned venison in large saucepan
• Cook egg noodles separately and add to venison
• Add a jar of gravy if desired
• Stir until hot and serve with your favorite rolls or bread

NEVER WASTE A ROAST
All roasts are not created equal, but all roasts are worth cooking. I usually remove the meat from neck roast before cooking because I am not a big fan of tallow. If cooked slowly, it can be quite tender and makes great sandwiches. Venison roasts make such a great meal to share; you don't want to waste a roast on a bad recipe.

(Rst) *Dr. Phillip & Brenda Bishop — The Aroma of Venison*

Our favorite recipe for venison is a double-double. It's a recipe that appeals to the nose first, and the palate later. It starts with a double amount of venison and results in a double dose of taste.

Sure enough…

Start with twice as much venison as you expect to eat. Place your venison in a slow cooker. Cover with your favorite marinade. Slow cook to taste. Enjoy the delicious aroma. Brenda likes it cooked until very tender; Phil prefers it a bit less cooked.

Slice and eat. It's as good cold as it is right out of the pot.

Now, what you haven't eaten, cut it up, or shred it. Put it back in the slow cooker, and cover with your favorite barbeque sauce. Heat. This makes the best barbeque sandwiches we have ever tasted.

In all honesty, we have a hard time deciding which we like more, the first serving, or the barbeque.

On second thought…maybe you ought to start with three times as much venison as you expect to eat.

BETTER THAN A SPORTS OR ENERGY DRINK?

When taken as a nutritional supplement, concentrated amounts of dried deer blood — obtained from crushed antler velvet — is believed to increase muscle tone and improve stamina and performance. According to Health Research Lab, a high-quality distributor of nutritional supplements, the supplement appears to be a safe and natural alternative to synthetic steroids.

(Rst) *Tom Carpenter's Sunday Afternoon Venison Pot Roast*

Once hunting season has wound down and Sunday (or Saturday!) afternoons free up for my family, it's time to re-live our hunts with venison pot roast. After tenderloins and backstraps, roasts are next to come off every deer we shoot. This recipe is not all that difficult to make, but you have to start early in the afternoon and get it in the oven. Then, after a little clean-up, we're free to watch some of the football we missed all fall because we were hunting (a good tradeoff), enjoy the smells of a house filling up with delicious aromas and reminisce about the deer cooking and ones yet to come.

Tips:
- Most any roast cut will do — either a front shoulder or from the rump area.
- Adjust amounts used — on venison and vegetables — to suit the size of group you're feeding.
- Don't be afraid to make the bouillon on the strong side.
- Serve with slices of crusty bread on the side.
- A hearty Merlot wine is a perfect accompaniment.

1 or 2 venison roasts, 2 to 3 pounds each	**beef bouillon**
flour	**celery (1 bunch)**
McCormick® Grill Mates® Montreal Steak Seasoning (or any salty/ peppery spice blend you like)	**onions (2 large)**
	small red potatoes (10)
rosemary	**parsnips**
vegetable oil	**carrots (1 pound)**
	fresh horseradish

Preheat oven to 400 degrees.

In skillet (preferably black cast iron), heat about 3/8-inch vegetable oil on medium heat. Season a cup or so of flour with spice blends. Roll roast(s) in flour blend, coating evenly. When oil is sizzling, brown roasts on all sides (might have to do roasts one at a time). Get a good crust. Set roasts aside. In same skillet, add some oil back in, then toss in onion that you have sliced and celery that you have chopped (include leaves). Sauté until onions are translucent, then transfer all vegetables and oil to a roasting pan. Make 2 cups of beef bouillon (or use canned beef stock) and put in roasting pan with vegetables. Put the roasts on the bed of vegetables and bouillon, cover with lid or aluminum foil and put in oven. Roast for about three hours. The foil or cover holds moisture in as the meat cooks. With one hour left, slice the potatoes in half and throw in, peel the parsnips and section them and throw in, and re-cover. With a half hour left, throw in carrots and re-cover. Remove covering for last 15 minutes or so and sprinkle all with a little bit of rosemary to taste. Provide fresh horseradish at the table as a condiment for the meat for those who can take the heat!

ⓢ *Jim & Ann Casada's*
Venison Loin Steaks with Crab, Shrimp & Scallop Sauce

This is a surf-and-turf recipe, which, while a bit demanding in terms of preparation, will grace the finest of tables in splendid style.

Serves: 4

1 pound loin steaks, cut 1/2" thick	1 tablespoon butter
1 tablespoon olive oil	salt & pepper to taste

Place olive oil and butter in a large skillet and quickly cook venison loin until medium-rare. Keep steaks warm on a platter. It is best to cook loin after sauce has started thickening.

Crab, Shrimp and Scallop Sauce

2 tablespoons olive oil	1/2 pound crabmeat
1/2 pound fresh mushrooms, sliced	8-12 medium shrimp, cooked and
2 cups whipping cream	shelled
1/4 cup white Zinfandel wine	6-8 sea scallops, cooked and
1/4 cup butter, cut into 12 pieces	chopped

Heat olive oil in a large skillet. Add mushrooms and sauté for five minutes. Add cream and wine and reduce until thickened (about 10-12 minutes). Season with salt and pepper. Stir in butter one piece at a time incorporating each piece completely before adding next. Add crabmeat, shrimp and scallops, heat through, for about one minute. Pour over venison. Serve immediately.

TIPS FOR STORING JERKY
According to the National Center for Home Food Preservation, properly prepared (dried) venison jerky will keep at room temperature two weeks in a sealed container. For best results, place your venison jerky in sealed glass or plastic container or zip-shut plastic bag and freeze or place in the refrigerator.

(Grd) *Jim & Ann Casada's Meatballs in Currant Sauce*

These meatballs make a great and hearty hors d'oeuvre, and they are the perfect foil to anyone who says "I don't like venison." They disappear like magic.

1-1/2 pounds ground venison	**1/4 cup finely minced onion**
1/2 cup dry bread crumbs	**1-1/2 teaspoons salt**
1/2 cup milk	**1/4 teaspoon pepper**
1 egg, beaten	**1/4 teaspoon garlic powder**

Mix ingredients well and shape into 1-inch balls. Place in a baking dish and brown in 350-degree oven for 30 minutes. Drain well if needed.

Heat a 10 oz jar of red currant jelly and a 12 oz jar of chili sauce in a large skillet. Add meatballs and simmer for 30 minutes. Serve hot in a chafing dish.

(Stk) *Gary Clancy's Almost World-Famous Baked Venison Steak*

Cut steaks 1-inch thick and then pound to 1/2-inch thickness. Season flour with salt, pepper or whatever you like and coat steaks on both sides. Brown steaks in a pan with hot butter. Remove steaks and pour in two beef bouillon cubes dissolved in a cup of hot water. Scrape the pan to get all of the crusty stuff mixed in with the bouillon and then put the steak back in the pan. On each steak, put a pad of butter and a level teaspoon of brown sugar. Liberally sprinkle chopped onions over the whole works and top off everything with ketchup. Bake in the oven at 350 degrees for 45 minutes. I cover it the first 30 minutes and take the cover off for the last 15.

To keep it simple, I serve with baked potatoes or sweet potatoes and often a squash. Put the spuds and squash in 15 minutes before the meat, and everything will be done at the same time.

KEEP IT SALTY

Whether it's whole-meat strips dried in a dehydrator or ground venison jerky made from a shooter, skimping on salt is not a recommended practice, according to the National Center for Home Food Preservation at the University of Georgia. Salt acts as a binding agent for moisture, which allows bacteria to be killed more quickly during the drying process.

(Stk) *Les & Connie Davenport's Marinade*

Raised in a family of six kids, we ate lots of wild game, mostly pheasant, rabbit, quail and squirrel. There were not many deer in our region of Illinois until the mid-1960s. I downed my first whitetail, an eight-point, in 1964, and quickly became addicted to the sport.

Shortly after marrying my wife, Connie, in August of 1970, I got a rude awakening. She could not cook wild game worth a hoot! Unlike my mother who always took great pains with wild game, Connie either overcooked or burnt it. It only took a couple of references to "This don't taste like Mom's" before things changed. Today, almost 40 years later, I would be hard pressed to find anyone who can cook venison — or any wild game — as well as Connie.

The initial key to good venison is, of course, the field-dressing process. Gutting and bleeding a deer immediately after the kill is essential. Deer that have been left in the field overnight often have the flavor of liver due to blood that coagulates in the veins. There is nothing wrong with liver … unless you are expecting the taste of steak.

Removing "all" the hair is also important to savory venison. It only requires one ground-up hair follicle to ruin the taste of an entire pound of hamburger. If you freeze venison burger or roasts for more than a few months, it is vital to remove as much of the deer fat as possible; it does not freeze as well as beef fat and eventually gives the meat a stale flavor.

Connie has taken even greater pride in preparing venison since taking up deer hunting in 1994. She has harvested nine deer in the past two seasons, six with bow and three with gun. Seems we supply half the neighborhood with deer of late. Here is one of Connie's marinade recipes for grilled venison. It is one of my absolute favorites! (By the way, after 39 years of marriage, the mother-thing does not work anymore.) Enjoy!

4 tablespoons cooking oil	**1/2 teaspoon pepper**
4 tablespoons soy sauce	**1/2 teaspoon vinegar**
2 tablespoons Worcestershire sauce	**small to medium onion diced fine**
3 tablespoons lemon juice	

Mix ingredients and microwave for three minutes. Pour hot marinate juice over meat and allow to cool in refrigerator for 24-48 hours (use the longer time for thicker meat). Use a meat thermometer for best results. Do not allow the meat to reach over 160 degrees Fahrenheit while grilling; it will dry out and lose its tenderness. This mix is great for backstrap steaks or skewed kabobs.

Ⓢⓣⓚ *Craig Dougherty's*
Butterflied Bacon-Wrapped Venison Loins

6-8 butterflied venison loins
3 oz steak sauce
1 oz soy sauce
1 oz Worcestershire sauce

pre-cooked bacon
Monterey Jack cheese
McCormick® Grill Mates® Montreal
  Steak Seasoning

Marinate six to eight butterflied venison loins in steak sauce, Worcestershire sauce and soy sauce. Let stand for at least four hours. Individually wrap each loin with pre-cooked bacon, adding a 1-inch piece of Monterey Jack cheese between the butterflied loins. Tightly wrap and place a toothpick through the loin to secure.
Grill: 10 – 16 minutes
Broil: 18 minutes at 450 degrees

Ⓢⓣⓚ *Mark & Tracy Drury's Grilled Whitetail Tenderloins*

Inside whitetail tenders or
  backstraps
Marinade ingredients:
1/2 cup water
1 cup cola

1 cup Dale's® seasoning, soy sauce
  or Teriyaki sauce
1 teaspoon liquid smoke
1 tablespoon brown sugar
2 tablespoons hickory brown sugar
  barbeque sauce

Soak tenders or backstraps in water in the refrigerator for two or three days, changing water frequently. This ages the meat all the while cleansing it of any gamey taste.
Freeze meat at least overnight to aid in the tenderizing process. Cut into small thin 1/4-inch slices while meat is still firm as it thaws. Marinate slices overnight in the combined marinade ingredients.
Grill over an open fire on low SLOWLY until meat is still red to very pink or to your likeness. Meat will melt in your mouth!

PINEAPPLE & VENISON = HEALTH FOODS
If you've read this far, you've realized the many health benefits associated with eating venison. Want to supercharge your healthy diet? Include modest portions of pineapple with every venison meal. Pineapple contains special enzymes that will help your digestive system break down the meat's fat, cholesterol and protein more easily. This allows your body to digest the food more quickly.

(Rst) *Pat & Penny Durkin's*
Teriyaki Marinade for Roasts or Shish-Kabobs

1/4 cup honey (or corn syrup)
1/4 cup vegetable oil
2 garlic cloves, minced
1/4 cup soy sauce
2 tablespoons vinegar

1 tablespoon grated fresh ginger root
2 tablespoons, minced onions
pepper (to preference)

After mixing ingredients, pour into a quart-size plastic bag and add venison roast or large cubes of venison for shish-kabobs. Seal and refrigerate at least 12 hours before grilling.

(Stk) *John Eberhart's Steak Recipe No. 1: Basic Fried Venison*

This is by far my favorite way to eat venison steak.

This recipe calls for cubed steak about 3/8-inch thick (cut all fat off before cooking). If you don't have a cuber, you can pound any cut of venison steak with a tenderizer until it is 3/8-inch thick.

Pour cooking oil (vegetable, canola or olive) in a 10-inch pan until the bottom of the pan is completely covered.

Place it on the stove over a medium low heat setting.

Roll the steaks in flour until completely covered.

Place steaks in pan once oil is hot.

Completely cover both sides of the steak in flour and place them in the pan.

Cook until the upper side of the steaks begins to turn color (about two to three minutes), flip them and turn the heat down as low as it will go.

Sprinkle on some McCormick® Grill Mates® Montreal Steak Seasoning (don't get carried away) and cover the pan with a lid.

Let simmer for about four minutes, remove from stove and eat.

THE TRUE THANKSGIVING DAY MEAT
Although most folks consider the turkey to be the star of the traditional Thanksgiving Day meal, historians note that the bird was most likely not available during the first meeting of the Colonial pilgrims and the American Indians. In fact, white-tailed deer venison was most likely the entrée served on that day, as it was the only readily available big-game animal in that region. Other foods that were likely served include duck, goose, corn, potatoes and wild roots.

(Stk) *John Eberhart's*
Steak Recipe No. 2: Terriyaki Quick Fried Venison

This recipe also calls for cubed steak about 3/8-inch thick (cut all fat off steaks before cooking). If you don't have a cuber, you can pound any cut of venison steak with a tenderizer until it is 3/8-inch thick. You will also need some sliced mushrooms.

Melt 1/3 stick of butter in a 10-inch pan on a medium low heat

Once melted, pour three tablespoons of Teriyaki marinade into the pan and mix it with the melted butter.

Put the sliced mushrooms into the pan, turn the heat up to medium, cover and let simmer for about 10 minutes (flipping the mushrooms every two minutes).

Once mushrooms are done, pour juice and mushrooms into a bowl.

Turn the heat back to medium low and melt another 1/3 stick of butter in the same pan, and once melted, pour another 3 tablespoons of Teriyaki marinade in and mix.

Once it starts to bubble, place the steaks (nothing on the steaks) in the mixed sauce, turn the heat down to low and cover.

Flip steaks after about three minutes and let simmer for another three minutes.

Remove steaks and cover with mushrooms and sauce.

(Grd) *John Eberhart's*
Steak Recipe No. 3: Swedish Venison Meatballs

Although it is a little difficult, this one's to die for.
This recipe calls for a bit of time and:

2 pounds of ground venison	**2 eggs**
4 tablespoons butter	**salt & lemon pepper**
1 cup chopped onion	**3 tablespoons flour**
1 cup bread crumbs	**2 cups of chicken broth**
1 cup milk	**2 cups of half 'n half or cream**

Melt 2 tablespoons of the butter in a large cooking pan and add the onion. Cook until onion is wilted. Pour onions and butter in a large mixing bowl and add the milk, bread crumbs, eggs, salt and lemon pepper (to liking), and ground venison, blend well. Shape into meatballs. Melt the other 2 tablespoons of butter in pan and add meatballs. Cook over gentle heat, turning carefully so they can brown evenly for about 10 minutes. Once brown, transfer them to a large saucepan. To the small amount of fat left in the cooking pan, add flour and stir. If there is no fat in pan, melt another 2 tablespoons of butter and mix before adding flour. Once flour is mixed in, add chicken broth while stirring. Simmer and stir for about a minute or so and add half 'n half while stirring and then let simmer for two minutes or longer.
Pour this sauce over meatballs in saucepan and bring to a slow boil. Ok, now you can eat!

(Stk) *Jake & Katie Edson's Bacon-Wrapped Backstrap*

6" to 8" cut of venison backstrap	6 strips of bacon
2 slices American cheese	1 tablespoon butter
1/2 green pepper, chopped	2 tablespoons seasoned salt
1/2 small onion, chopped	1 cup teriyaki marinade
1 small can mushroom pieces	

Sweat onion and green pepper in a small frying pan with butter until both are tender. Drain mushrooms and add to pan, then remove from heat. Meanwhile, trim fat and silver skin from the loin and cut into the center lengthwise to create a pocket for the vegetable mixture. Coat venison liberally with seasoning salt inside and out, then stuff with onion/mushroom/green pepper mixture and cheese, then close opening. Place bacon strips on a cutting board next to each other and lay venison across the strips. Wrap bacon strips around the backstrap, overlapping the ends.

Marinade in Teriyaki for one hour.

Remove from marinade and place on a grill at low heat and cook for eight to 10 minutes per side. When the bacon is crispy, the meat should be cooked to medium-rare.

(Rst) *Glenn & Judy Helgeland's Marinated Venison Roast*

This marinade is also good with any white meat, like chicken, turkey, pork and game birds. Be sure to serve with something to soak up the marinade.

Serves: 4-6

1 1/2 pounds venison round steak	1 1/2 teaspoons lemon juice
4 tablespoons low salt soy sauce	4 tablespoons red wine vinegar
2 tablespoons salad oil	1 clove garlic, crushed
2 tablespoons Worcestershire sauce	1/4 pound diced bacon

Cut the meat into bite size pieces and add meat and marinade to a 1 gallon, self-sealing plastic bag. Marinate for at least 30 minutes and up to four hours, turning meat and marinade several times in the refrigerator.

Heat an electric skillet to 275 degrees. Brown the bacon pieces and remove from the skillet. Add the meat and marinade and cook for about 45 minutes, being sure not to overcook the meat. Add the bacon pieces and serve.

MEAT GRINDER TIPS, PART I

Contrary to popular belief, running bread through your meat grinder is not an effective means of cleaning it. Bread will introduce more bacteria into the equipment, which poses future health hazards. Instead, clean your grinder with extremely hot, soapy water. This will help breakdown fat residue from deer tallow. Next, run a piper cleaner or similar small wire through the holes of the screen to remove all debris. Rinse all equipment with hot water, and dry with paper toweling.

Grd *Dave & Debbie Henderson's Venison Chili*

Adapting ideas from writer buddy Mike Bleech, a certified chili-making champion in Pennsylvania, we've come up with a family favorite that can be changed (sweet, hot, mild, etc.) to our preferences at the time. Mike says that real chili cooks don't use chili mixes, ground meat or beans. Chopped venison (1/4-inch pieces) does, indeed, make for a more flavorful dish with appealing texture, but it is also labor intensive. Beans are always optional here, depending on whether we're on a low-carbohydrate diet at the time.

4 pounds of venison (chopped or ground)

1 can (8 oz) of beans (kidney, black, white, Cajun, chili, etc.) of your choice

3 tablespoons McCormick® Mexican (hot or regular) Chili Powder

1 teaspoon cumin

3 teaspoons hot pepper sauce (or salt, pepper and hot sauce)

3 tablespoons Worcestershire or soy sauce (low sodium if you prefer)

1 tablespoon garlic juice or salt

1 onion (Vidalia if you want it sweet)

1 pepper (green for hot or mild; yellow or red for sweet)

1 tablespoon brown sugar (brown sugar alternative if you prefer)

1 8 oz can tomato sauce or diced tomatoes

1 6 oz can tomato paste

Brown meat in pot, with 1/4 cup of olive oil, over very low flame and add all ingredients except tomato paste and sauce. Since venison is very lean, some people add water or beef bouillon. Stir frequently.

Flame height is critical. Should be just high enough to bubble the mixture lightly. Anymore and the juice evaporates.

After two hours, add tomato sauce (or diced) and let simmer for another one and a half hours. Timing should give flavors time to blend perfectly. If it's too spicy, add grated cheese.

MEAT GRINDER TIPS, PART II

After washing and drying your meat grinder and its accessories, hang-dry all metal parts. One method that works well is to hang the parts near a woodstove to dry evenly and quickly. When this is not possible, a hair dryer will suffice. Do not lay the grinder or accessories on their side to dry; they will rust if you do. Coat all metal parts with a fine application of commercial-grade grinder oil. Do not use vegetable oil or any petroleum-based product. Before storing, wrap dry parts in clean, dry paper toweling.

(Stk) *Kevin Howard's Skillet Venison Steak 'N' Potatoes*

Variation: This recipe can also be cooked in a slow cooker. After steak is browned in the skillet, put broth, water and thicker slices of potatoes and half of the onion in the slow cooker. Place the browned meat on top and then the rest of the potatoes and onion. You can layer the meat in if you need to. Cook on high for five hours or on low for eight-10 hours.

Serves: 6

1-1/2 pound boneless round steak, cut 1/2" thick, trimmed	2 tablespoons vegetable oil
	1 10-1/2 oz can beef broth, undiluted
1/4 cup flour	1 cup water
2 teaspoons salt	4 medium potatoes, thinly sliced
1/4 teaspoon pepper	2 medium onions, thinly sliced

Cut steak into serving-size pieces. If it is from an older deer, tenderized. Soak meat overnight in milk.

Combine flour, salt and pepper. Dredge steak in flour mixture.

Brown steak on both sides in hot oil in a medium to large iron skillet.

Add broth and water; cover and simmer for 30 minutes.

Turn meat and top with potatoes and onion.

Cover and simmer for 20 minutes or until potatoes are done.

(Stk) *Kevin Howard's Grilled Venison Loin Steaks*

This is a great and easy way to prepare venison loin in camp.

Serves: 4

2 pounds venison loin	Cavender's® All Purpose
olive oil	Greek seasoning (www. greekseasoning.com)

Cut loin into 1- thick steaks, tenderize and soak in milk for a couple of hours or more. Drain steaks and pat dry. Coat steaks with olive oil and then season each side with Cavender's® All Purpose Greek seasoning. Grill over high heat for three to four minutes per side. Serve medium rare to medium. Don't over overcook.

REAL MEN EAT VENISON, PART I

"Once or twice, however, while I lived at the pond, I found myself ranging the woods, like a half-starved hound, with a strange abandonment, seeking some kind of venison which I might devour, and no morsel could have been too savage for me."
— Henry David Thoreau, *Walden*, 1845-1849

(Rst) *Tes & Ron Jolly's Venison Spread*

Like many good family recipes handed down through the generations, this one gets tweaked according to the cook's tastes. Good hunting! — Tes Jolly

Cut 3 pounds of venison into large chunks and place in slow cooker or soup pot. Chop one medium onion, add to pot. Add 1 tablespoon salt. Add water to cover. Bring to a boil, then cover and simmer till tender. Remove meat and cool.

Discard onion and broth or, better yet, feed it to your pet.

Grind a sweet medium-sized onion with the meat using a coarse grinder blade. Put meat/onion mixture in a large bowl. Add 1 cup (more or less to taste) sweet pickle relish. Toss together. In a separate bowl, mix: 1 cup each mayonnaise and light non-mayonaise-type salad dressing spread, 1/4 cup cider vinegar, 2 tablespoons (to taste) horseradish sauce, 1/2 cup sugar, 1 or 2 tablespoons yellow mustard. Add mayo/salad dressing mixture to the meat mixture. Stir to blend. If the mixture is too dry, prepare additional dressing and add to taste.

Serve with cracker, chips, bread or a fork! Here's another tip: For those whose like a little kick, add chopped jalapenos to the mix.

(Stk) *Don Kirk's Hinny BBQ*

This has become a favorite during football season. If you like tender, juicy chopped or sliced BBQ, this is the ticket. The biggest key is having an infrared cooker. Propane powered, it allows you to cook whole turkeys that come out as though they are deep fried, but it is all infrared heat.

Hindquarter of venison with bone in, trimmed of fat and bottom portion of leg removed.	**12 oz buttermilk**
	5 oz extra virgin olive oil
	1 pound brisket rub
32 oz orange juice	

Combine orange juice, buttermilk, olive oil and 1 cup of rub in a large plastic or glass container large enough to these ingredients and the hind quarter of venison. Never, and I repeat never, use an aluminum container for this or any other marinade. Refrigerate for no less than 4 hours, and no more than 6. Any longer makes the meat mushy. Before cooking, dry the hindquarter with paper towel. Once dry, apply the remainder of your rub. Place in basket to cook. Allow 8 minutes per pound to cook. So easy that even a caveman can do it.

REAL MEN EAT VENISON, PART II
"A man who in civilization would be merely a backbiter becomes a murderer on the frontier; and, on the other hand, he who in the city would do nothing more than bid you a cheery good-morning, shares his last bit of sun-jerked venison with you when threatened by starvation in the wilderness." — Theodore Roosevelt, "Frontier Types," 1888.

(Rst) *Walt Larsen's Shredded Barbecue Vension*

1 venison roast (about 3 pounds);
  cut into steak-sized pieces
1 teaspoon celery salt

1 teaspoon garlic powder
1 teaspoon onion powder
18 oz barbeque sauce

Place a large piece of tin foil in slow cooker. Combine celery salt, garlic powder and onion powder; rub over roast. Place meat in the foil and add 1/2 cup water to meat. Close foil in top. Cover and cook on low six to eight hours or until meat is tender.

Remove roast and cool slightly. Strain cooking juices, reserving 1/2 cup. Shred meat with two forks; place in a large saucepan. Add the barbeque sauce and reserved cooking juices; heat through. Serve on buns.

(Stk) *Mike Mattly's Backstraps*

Here is an easy recipe that we use for deer, antelope or elk backstraps. Since it is hard for me to cook a fillet and have it medium-medium rare throughout, I like to make kabobs. We especially like to cook these when we go out on the boat for the shore lunch. I have been able to get all of our friend's wives and kids to even ask for venison kabobs!

green pepper
yellow pepper
red onion
small whole mushrooms
venison backstraps
Merlot wine
Italian salad dressing

Teriyaki sauce
Worcestershire sauce
Cavender's® All Purpose
  Greek seasoning or your
  favorite steak seasoning
  (www.greekseasoning.com)
raspberry vinaigrette salad dressing

I cut all the meat into bite sized pieces making sure to remove all the silver skin and any gristle.

Mix equal portions of merlot, Italian salad dressing and teriyaki in a bowl for steak marinade. Sprinkle in Cavender's® and a few dashes of Worcestershire. I put the meat in a gallon-size resealable plastic bag and pour in the marinade. Close the seal and shake the contents to get the marinade on all of the meat. Put in the fridge overnight.

Cut up all the veggies. Mix equal parts for a marinade of: merlot and raspberry vinaigrette. Put veggies and this marinade in a resealable plastic bag and put in fridge overnight.

Skewer and grill or you can cook in a wok. I like to put down aluminum foil on the grill to keep the flames from charring the meat and veggies. Serve immediately, because the meat will dry out.

Ⓢ Ⓖ *Ted & Shemane Nugent's*
Bubble Bean Piranha-Ala-Colorado Moose

The last pure, perfect positive environmental function available to mankind is to be the ultimate conscientious consumer by hunting, fishing and trapping God's natural annual surplus. Like all American hunters, the Nugent family takes this responsibility seriously, and the higher level of awareness learned through this natural, reasoning predator duty forces us to treat each gift of protein with the respect and reverence it deserves. This spiritual rocket fuel is not only the healthiest food on the planet, it is also the most delicious. A hunter is compelled to handle this sacred flesh with tender loving care, and the final meal is always very special. Plus, when I go crazy in the kitchen, everybody has a good time.

This is it, folks! The chow the whole world has been waitin' for! Proven at the hands of the most voracious of camphogs, this rib-stickin' slop is the ultimate in hunt camp fortification. As the primary mainstay at the Nugent Whackmaster Strap Assassin Headquarters, many a hearty hunter has maintained the killer instinct by gettin' a belly full of my primo-extremo predator brew. First experimented with as early as 1968, the recipe has changed little over the years, but rather improved with the spirit of adventure.

This sacred Backstrap celebration courtesy of Tednugent.com.

Serves about 5 average folk, or two major Nuge camp swine.

1 pound ground venison (any)	**1 large box pasta noodles (elbows**
1 deer backstrap	**or sea shells)**
2 green peppers	**cayenne pepper**
2 red peppers	**Mrs. Dash® Original Blend**
1 large sweet onion	**McCormick® Grill Mates® Montreal**
1 large white or red onion	**Steak Seasoning**
1 bunch scallions	**1/2 pound butter**
1 large bowl fresh mushrooms	**1/4 cup olive oil**
1 whole clove garlic	

In a skillet, brown the ground meat. Dice all the vegetables into bite sized chunks. Add half of the vegetables to the browned meat. Boil the pasta and drain. Singe the backstrap in bite-size pieces in hot olive oil. Squash and add the garlic to the browned meat and vegetables. Stir vigorously. Throw the whole load into a large pot on low heat, including the remaining raw vegetables. Still stirring, add small amounts of water to desired consistency. Keep on lowest heat all day. Refrigerate overnight and reheat for days to come. It's best two to three days old. Slop a load onto bread, mashed potatoes, rice or serve by itself. Throw a log on the fire, kick back, relax and swap hunting lies.

⟨Stk⟩ *Ted & Shemane Nugent's Venison Stroganoff*

Recipe from Kill It and Grill It (Regnery: $16.95).

2 pounds venison steaks
1 envelope onion soup mix
fresh mushrooms
1 beef bouillon cube
cooking Sherry

1 cup sour cream
curry powder
garlic salt

Cut meat in thin strips (eliminating fat). Brown quickly in 3 tablespoons or more butter with mushrooms. Stir in 2/3-cup liquid (1/3 water, 1/3 sherry). Add the onion soup mix, a dash of garlic salt, a dash of curry powder, and the bouillon cube. Mix well, cover and simmer for one to two hours or until meat is tender. Stir every 15 minutes, adding liquid when necessary. Just before serving, add sour cream and increase heat. Serve over rice or noodles for four unless Ted's eating over, then it'll serve two.

⟨Stk⟩ *Zeke Pipher's Venison Risotto with Red Wine*

1-1/2 pounds venison, cut into
  1-inch cubes (backstrap or
  tenderloin)
1 cup red wine (a dry red, such as
  a Zinfandel, Cabernet Sauvignon,
  or Merlot)
3 cups Arborio rice
8 cups of chicken stock

3/4 cup of extra-virgin olive oil
1/2 cup chopped white onion
1/2 cup sliced celery
1/2 cup chopped Portobello
  mushrooms
3 tablespoons unsalted butter
1/2 cup grated Parmesan cheese
salt and pepper

You'll need two large saucepans. In the first saucepan, bring the chicken stock to boil, reduce heat and leave at a gentle simmer. In the second saucepan, heat 1/2 cup of olive oil (medium heat) and then add onion, celery and mushrooms. Sauté until these ingredients soften, approximately six to eight minutes. Add the venison and continue to sauté until the meat is browned, approximately six to eight minutes.

Remove the meat and the other ingredients from the saucepan. Add back 1/4 cup of olive oil and then pour in the rice. Brown the rice, stirring frequently, until it begins to change to a clear color, approximately five minutes. Add the dry red wine and stir until the wine is completely absorbed by the rice.

Begin adding the chicken stock, 1 cup at a time. Stir frequently after each cup. When the stock has almost absorbed but not completely, add the next cup of stock, stirring frequently. After several cups, the rice will begin to appear creamy, approximately 15 minutes. The outside of the rice will appear soft, but the inside will still have a slight crunch to it. It is at this point that you add the beef and vegetables back to the saucepan. Continue to add the stock and stir frequently.

When the rice is creamy and tastes soft, add the butter and Parmesan cheese. Salt and pepper to taste. When the butter is melted, serve immediately.

ⓢ *Bob Robb's French Pepper Venison Steak Kabobs*

4 12- to 16-oz. venison backstrap steaks
 or tenderloins
2 cups soy sauce
1/4 cup lime juice
2 cups flour
3/4 cup coarse-ground black pepper
 mixed into 2 cups brown
Burgundy Sauce

corn oil
8 tomato wedges
8 bell pepper wedges
 (green, red or yellow)
8 onion wedges
6 cups cooked wild rice

Preheat oven to 500 degrees.

Burgundy Sauce — made from four cups of beef stock, Burgundy wine to taste, and enough flour to thicken to your taste.

Chunk each piece of venison into six pieces. Mix soy and lime juice. Mix flour and 1/2 cup coarse ground pepper. Put about 1/4-inch of corn oil into a hot skillet and heat it until it pops when a drop of water is dropped into it. Place tomato, bell pepper and onion wedges in a roasting pan and cook them in the oven for five to 10 minutes at 350 degrees, timing it so they are done at the same time the steak pieces are. Using tongs, dip steak chunks into the soy-lime juice mixture, then into the flour mixture, coating them on all sides. Handle venison pieces as to not knock off the flour. The key is to cook the meat on all sides, creating a light crust. After coating, fry the meat in the skillet, raising the meat after the first minute of cooking so the oil runs beneath the chunks. When it is golden brown and the meat is not overcooked, remove and gently pat it down with paper towels to remove excess oil. Spread cooked rice on dinner plates and place the meat on top of the rice, gently pouring the Burgundy Sauce over them. Arrange the cooked vegetables around the edges and voila! Bon Appetite.

FLUKES WON'T RUIN THE CELEBRATION

Fried venison liver is not only a delicacy but an opening-day tradition in deer camps across North America. The presence of liver flukes has caused many hunters to give up this tradition — and eating liver altogether — both of which are unnecessary measures, according to wildlife biologists. The trematode that is frequently found in venison liver is actually a large American liver fluke. It resembles a long, flat worm or a purplish-gray leech. Flukes are often surrounded by a fibrous capsule. Unsightly? Yes. Harmful to your health? No. According to the researchers at the Michigan Department of Natural Resources, "This parasite is not infective for humans and presents no public health menace. The main prohibition against human consumption of cooked deer liver containing flukes would be an aesthetic one."

(Rst) *Chrisanthia Schmidt's Venison Pot Roast*

Serves: 6

1 boneless shoulder 3-4 pound
  venison roast
3 tablespoons vegetable oil
1 14 oz can chicken broth

1/3 cup soy sauce
1 onion, quartered
4 cloves garlic, minced
1/2 teaspoon ground ginger

In a Dutch oven brown, roast in oil then add next five ingredients. Cover and simmer four hours.

(Rst) *Chrisanthia Schmidt's Venison Roast Teriyaki*

Serves: 6

1 boneless 3-4 pound venison roast
1 cup white wine plus 1/2 cup more
  for marinade, divided
1 package onion soup mix
1/2 cup plus 2 tablespoons Teriyaki
  sauce

2 onions, chopped
1 pound fresh mushrooms
4 carrots, sliced
5 red potatoes, peeled and sliced

Place roast into plastic food bag. Pour wine over roast and seal bag. Refrigerate in marinade for four hours. Remove roast from bag and discard bag. Combine 1 cup wine, soup mix and Teriyaki. Place roast and onions in roast pan, cover with wine mixture. Bake at 300 degrees for one hour then add mushrooms, carrots and potatoes. Reduce heat to 275 degrees and bake 1-1/2 hours or until meat is tender.

(Stk) *Dan Schmidt's One-Shot Backstraps*

This is Dan's favorite way to make fresh backstraps.

venison backstrap steaks
2 tablespoons butter

2 cloves garlic, minced
1/4 small onion, diced

In skillet, heat butter. Add onion and garlic, sauté until soft but not brown, add backstraps and sear on both sides. Continue cooking until desired doneness is reached, maybe a minute or two on each side.

GET AN OIL CHANGE
  Healthy eating doesn't mean that you have to give up on pan-fried foods like venison tenderloin. If butter and vegetable oil are on your do-not-eat list, consider switching to olive oil. This all-natural cooking wonder is high in healthy monounsaturated fatty acids and high in antioxidants. In fact, scientific studies have shown that olive oil helps control "bad" (LDL) cholesterol levels while raising "good" (HDL) cholesterol levels.

Blood Trailing & Equipment Tips

by Daniel E. Schmidt, Editor, *Deer & Deer Hunting*

1. The Key to Finding Blood

The key to finding "first blood" is knowing exactly where the deer was standing when you released the shot and pinpointing the exact spot where you last saw the deer. Sounds simple. However, many hunters fail to mentally record these details, and experience difficulties after climbing down from their stands.

2. Appoint a Team Leader

Leadership and organization is essential when successfully trailing wounded deer. It is key to have one person calling the shots. It could be the hunter who shot the deer. It could be the hunter with the most experience. Whoever it is, that person needs to be patient and meticulous. Whatever he says goes. No ifs, ands or buts.

3. Take Control

When blood trailing, three's a crowd. Only allow a third person to enter the blood-trailing picture when a difficult trail requires a roamer. This tracker carefully circles ahead of a lost trail in hopes of relocating blood sign. This person must be willing to take detailed instruction from the team leader, because they can easily disturb previously unseen blood, scuff marks from hoof prints, overturned leaves, etc.

4. Mark Your Trail

No matter how short or easy you think a blood trail will be, play it safe from the start by marking key evidence. Place small pieces (2-inch squares) of biodegradable toilet paper next to the first sign of blood, scuff marks, hair, etc. Keep the trail going until you've found your deer. This tactic will help you unravel tricky trails, especially if a deer "doubles back" on its track.

5. Never Assume

Trailing a wounded deer is not the time to "try to think like a deer." This approach seldom works, because wounded deer often exhibit unpredictable behavior. Blood trailing requires meticulous attention to detail. If you want fresh venison backstraps for dinner, get on your hands and knees and look for sign; don't try to guess what the deer did next.

6. Don't Underestimate Coyotes

If your deer hunting property is also home to coyotes and/or wolves, consider trailing every deer (except gut-shots) without much delay. A good rule of thumb is to wait at least an hour after shooting a deer while bowhunting. Waiting longer than that in coyote country, especially at night, will increase the chances that a mortally wounded deer will be lost to scavengers.

7. Don't Skimp on Lights

A single drop of blood is often the difference between finding your deer immediately and calling off the effort until daylight. The best lights to use are those that emit diffused rays that are consistent and bright. The best lights we've used over the years include lanterns, headlamps and handheld flashlights. We have not had success with lights featuring blue filters or the liquid-spray products that supposedly make blood appear brighter.

8. The Bigger They Are...

Deer are big animals, and the bigger they are, the harder they fall. According to researchers, a white-tailed deer's circulatory system contains 1 ounce of blood for every pound of body mass. Researchers have also concluded that a deer must lose one-third of its blood volume before it will die. On a big, mature buck, that might equate to as much as 5 pints.

9. Use a Compass

A simple compass reading just after the shot can point you in a straight line toward your dead deer. Many hunters simply use the sun's position in the sky for direction. That can provide a ballpark estimate, but it is not nearly as reliable as a precise compass reading.

10. Blood Identification: Lungs

Identifying blood from a single or double-lung wound is among the easiest things to do in deer hunting. The telltale signs of a lung hit are the presence of blood that appears pink and contains air bubbles (oxygen). Pure double-lung hits will often result in frothy blood sign that retains the consistency of a milkshake. Be warned: The mere presence of air bubbles does not always indicate a lung hit. Bubbles can also be introduced through partial lung hits, liver hits and esophagus and throat wounds.

11. Blood Identification: Liver

Substantial liver wounds in deer produce massive bleeding and a telltale bloodtrail featuring extremely dark red, almost maroon-colored blood sign. The liver sits vertically in back of a deer's stomach cavity — against the diaphragm. Because the liver also sits adjacent to the paunch, it is common for bowhunters to hit the liver and paunch/intestines on a quartering shot. A white-tailed deer will die quickly from a liver wound. However, it is wise to wait at least one hour before trailing the deer.

12. *Blood Identification: Paunch*

Paunch-shot deer are among the toughest to trail, but with a little experience the novice hunter will soon learn how to find every deer he or she shoots. The key to any "gut" shot deer (which includes paunch and intestine wounds), is to stay off of the blood trail for a minimum of 10 hours. Our family's rule is 12 hours. There really are no exceptions to this rule, because if you jump a gut-wounded deer from its bed, it will become exponentially harder to recover. Blood sign includes brownish discharge mixed in with the blood and bits or clumps of undigested foodstuffs from the paunch cavity.

13. *Blood Identification: Intestines*

Blood signs from intestinal wounds are similar to those from paunch wounds. The key difference is foodstuffs are mostly digested and result in brownish liquid instead of food matter on the trail. Because few veins and arteries run through this part of the deer, blood sign will result in the scarce drop-here-drop-there trail. Clues that indicate a gut wound include the deer hunching up at the shot and walking — not running — away. If you suspect an intestinal wound, wait at least 10 hours before taking up the trail.

14. *Blood Identification: Muscles*

Wounds to a deer's shoulder, legs or hindquarters will invariably produce bright-red blood trails. Muscle wounds also commonly produce trails that start off strong — with seemingly massive amounts of blood for 50 to 75 yards — then peter out to a single blood drop here and there. Unless the muscle wound is accompanied with a broken bone, the deer will likely survive and become older and smarter. Scientific research has shown that high volumes of Vitamin K-12 in deer blood promotes amazing recovery times from such superficial wounds.

15. *Blood Identification: Esophagus*

Bullet wounds to the throat almost always produce instant kills because of the resulting shock to the spinal column. Arrow wounds are a different story. Hitting the ½-inch wide esophagus, though rare, can result in a difficult to follow bloodtrail. The good news is the deer rarely goes far before dying. Blood sign is usually scant, but other sign, including white foam, greenish/yellow slime will indicate an esophagus wound. A mature white-tailed deer's esophagus measures about 24 inches long.

16. *Determine the Bloodtrail's Direction*

So, you found your deer's bloodtrail but now you're not sure which direction it's going? Don't despair. The biggest challenge in deer hunting is trailing a deer that's suddenly reversed its direction. To unravel it, get on your hands and knees and examine each drop, spray and smear of blood for a 5-yard section. Be careful not to step on the blood sign, as it will reveal telltale clues. Examine the drops of blood that hit the forest floor and note the tiny "spray" lines it left. Each drop should resemble a spider web of sorts. The spray lines will point you in the direction the deer was moving when the droplet hit the ground.

17. Know Which Cavity You're Dealing With

The key to knowing when to trail a deer and when to back off and wait is knowing precisely which cavity your bullet or arrow passed through. Shots to the chest cavity invariably lead to quick, clean kills. The chest cavity houses the deer's heart, lungs and esophagus. It is separated by the diaphragm. The stomach cavity houses the deer's liver, rumen and intestines. It is best to wait at least one hour before trailing a liver-shot deer and at least 10 hours before trailing a gut-shot deer.

18. Deer Behavior and Hypovolemic Shock

Experienced deer hunters know that wounded whitetails often seek water sources such as creeks, rivers, ponds and lakes. Old-time thinking was that deer sought wet areas because of the cooler temperatures and thicker cover. This is probably somewhat true, but researchers have concluded that wounded deer primarily seek water in an effort to replenish a loss of blood volume and the resulting low blood pressure in their circulatory systems that is caused by hypovolemic shock.

19. Few Deer Survive Bow-Shots

The word "never" should be left out of any deer hunter's vocabulary — except in the case of blood-trailing. For example, a hunter should never assume that his shot didn't kill the deer he or she was shooting at. According to a scientific study conducted by the Minnesota Department of Natural Resources, archers retrieve 86.8 percent of the deer they shoot. Although the remaining 13.2 percent figure seems high, this figure only indicates how many deer were not found. The researchers also concluded that a high number of the remains of unrecovered deer were found weeks and months later after scavengers had picked over the carcasses.

20. Why Archers Need a Razor's Edge

Unlike a bullet — which kills a deer through massive damage and shock — a broadhead does its job by surgically cutting tissue and inflicting massive hemorrhaging. The broadhead's sharpness is especially important when it comes in contact with a major artery. Deer arteries, including the aortic, carotid and femoral, are tough, yet elastic. This elasticity allows the artery to maintain constant blood pressure. View the artery as a large, thick rubber band. Is your broadhead sharp enough to sever it instantly?

Index

Ground

Ring Bologna

Roast

Sausage

Steak